RED FLAGS
DON'T FADE

THE ESSENTIAL RULES
FOR GUIDING
YOUR CHOICES

EVE ROSENBERG

© 2025 by Eve Rosenberg

All rights reserved. No part of this book may be reproduced in whole or part, or stored in a retrieval system, with the exception of brief quotations embodied in critical articles or reviews, or transmitted in any form or by any means, electronic, mechanical, photocopying, recording, or otherwise, without the written permission of the author. Requests for permission should be addressed in writing to the author at Eve@lessonslearnedinlove.com.

ISBN: 979-8-9993010-4-8 (Hardcover)
ISBN: 979-8-9993010-7-9 (Paperback)
ISBN: 979-8-9993010-9-3 (eBook)
Library of Congress Control Number: 2025913156
Printed in Delray Beach, Florida, USA by Eve Rosenberg

DISCLAIMER
This book is designed to provide general educational information about the topics discussed and not to diagnose, treat, cure, or prevent any psychological or emotional condition. It is not intended as a substitute for any diagnosis or treatment recommended by the readers' psychiatrist, psychologist, or any other medical practitioner. Use of this book does not establish any doctor-patient relationship between the reader and the author or publisher.

The author does not assume and hereby disclaims any liability to any party for any loss, damage, or disruption caused by errors or omissions, whether such errors or omissions result from accident, negligence, or any other cause. No warranties or guarantees are expressed or implied by their choice of content for this volume and there is no guarantee that these materials are suitable for the readers' particular purpose or situation. If you suspect you have a psychological or emotional problem, we urge you to seek help from the appropriate specialist. This book is not intended to be a substitute for the advice of a licensed physician or mental health provider.

Readers must rely on their own judgment about their circumstances and take full responsibility for all actions and decisions made because of reading this book and applying the recommended practices.

The author has made every effort to ensure the accuracy of the information within this book was correct at the time of publication. Any perceived slights of specific persons, peoples, or organizations are unintended. All names have been changed and any reference to a specific story or instance is coincidental.

For more information, visit www.howtobelieveinyou.com or email the author at Eve@lessonslearnedinlove.com.

To all the people who turn
away from their guidance,
may you find your way within.
and
To my father, Leslie,
for being my greatest teacher
and most profound love.

ACKNOWLEDGEMENTS

To my twin sister, Judy Legare, my wombmate and most profound teacher. I am cheering you on.

To my cousin, Vivian Chinelli, I love our discussions about synchronicities and Red Flags. I am so grateful we bonded during the insanity.

To Arlene, aka Red, an Angel in Heaven, I miss you, love you, and still hear your sound advice.

To a great teacher and mentor, the late Debbie Ford, my gratitude has no bounds.

To my friends whom I love dearly; you know who you are. Thank you for all your support and faith in me. You fill me with joy.

To my Fur Babies, Priscilla and Misty May Morning, thank you for your patience, tolerance, and company for all the hours it took to get this book done. Treats are imminent.

To my Publisher, Diana Needham at Business Book Partners; without your support none of my books would exist. My gratitude is infinite.

To my Cover Designer, Nathan Dasco, thank you for bringing my vision to life.

To my Proofreader, Rich Nichol, thank you for your finishing touches.

Hoisted atop a towering pole,
a vision our mind can't erase.
The crimson cloth waving
vies for our attention,
a warning we don't want to face.
Turning away will lead us astray.
Make sure you stop and listen.
There is information for you,
a direction or two,
the guidance until now you've been missing.
For all the efforts and choices you've made.
Always remember that Red Flags don't fade.

TABLE OF CONTENTS

A Note to the Reader ix
Introduction xi
Choices 1
Red Flags 11
The Missed Guidance 49
The Unreachable Dream 65
The Essential Rules 73
The After Party. 179

A NOTE TO THE READER

I don't know your personal history, but I suspect no matter what it is, that you too have experienced Red Flags showing up every now and then, or worse, in the most inopportune times of your life. Perhaps when happily coasting along, believing you have finally arrived somewhere good, there it is! Another Red Flag!

If you're like me, you may spot them as evidence of a hunch you've suspected, claiming a personal victory. Or you may question them, turn your back on them, or deny them, especially if they interfere with what you'd rather not know. You find yourself rationalizing, justifying, and convincing yourself these Red Flags don't pertain to *your* situation, that maybe it's *you* who is negative, critical, and untrusting. So, you decide to have faith and pretend you weren't warned.

No matter where Red Flags pop up in your life, I am here to inform and encourage you to see them as the best guidance available for directing your life with ease and clarity. Imagine a reputable psychic predicting your future or possessing a crystal ball with magical powers. Red Flags will support you in making the best choices for you.

Why?

Because Red Flags come from within you, your acquired knowledge and experience, and, I strongly suggest, from your gut and intuition as well. You wouldn't see Red Flags for the warnings they are unless they strike a familiar chord, or your gut is nudging you that something is off.

We are each connected to an inner being, a higher self, a source where we hold our core values and beliefs. Our thoughts, emotions and actions, and what truly matters to us are either aligned, *in harmony with*, or unaligned, *in dissonance with* our source. And when we experience Red Flags, we can shift from harmony to dissonance in an instant.

By following your inner voice, trusting what you feel and see (and I am not referring to touch and sight), the guidance that comes to you and through you is evidence that it's time to stop, pause, listen, and evaluate.

And, since structure is supportive and effective, I have created Essential Rules to help you with the process of heeding the Red Flags that vie for your attention, so that you can interpret and apply them, ensuring you make the best choices for *you* and *your* life. So, let's get started. The sooner you follow the Rules, the closer you are to living your best life.

INTRODUCTION

Creating this book has been a heart-driven process. A journey compelling enough to interrupt deep sleep; flooding my mind with profound insights, disrupting my dreams, and waking me with the urgency to write about Red Flags.

These strong nudges have come before, and whenever they do, I take *them* seriously.

I have learned in the past that following my gut is essential for living my greatest life and for producing my best work.

I am particularly proud of my last book, *My Dearest Self, I Forgive You*, a guide I desperately needed. A compilation of reminders of my inherent worth, it's an empowering gem that keeps giving without losing its value. It remains on my nightstand since its 2023 publication, and each time I pick it up, it delivers a potent dose of strength and confidence. Self-forgiveness is a soothing balm for the soul.

I thought it ironic though and chuckled how a book on Red Flags would follow a book on self-forgiveness, acknowledging it would make sense the latter preceded the former. Who doesn't need to forgive themselves for ignoring Red Flags and making bad choices?

But with careful introspection, I realized it was the self-forgiveness process that supported many of my memories returning; hence the Red Flags warehoused from long ago resurfacing, becoming crystal clear in present time. As the adage goes, *Hindsight is 20/20*. But hang on. I will challenge this expression in a later chapter when I discuss how Red Flags affect our choices.

I was flabbergasted then, when at the most inopportune times and without warning, I would receive a *hit*, the term I use to refer to sudden insights that come unexpectedly, bringing clarity and closure to an experience that was previously confusing or unresolved.

When such an experience befell me as I was washing dishes in my kitchen one afternoon, my heart took a nosedive to my stomach the instant the realization struck me. I shouted loud enough to startle my dog who was quietly nestled in her bed.

"Oh my gosh! He was cheating on me the entire relationship!"

Referring to my college boyfriend, Lloyd, whom I dated for close to four years and broke up with abruptly in my senior year when I discovered he was cheating on me, I now know with certainty that he wasn't loyal at all. What at first seemed like an isolated incident was instead a pattern and there were many Red Flags to support this. Instead of trusting the warnings, I put my faith in Lloyd.

To reiterate how powerful this guidance is, it was the nudge in my gut, a Red Flag alerting me during an intimate session with Lloyd, that exposed the betrayal. I had no concrete evidence except for the suspicions I felt when Lloyd bestowed his newly seductive Don Juan moves on me. I had to wonder who the experienced teacher was he learned from. This sparked the dreaded question.

"Lloyd, are you seeing other people?"

Lloyd got defensive and used his gaslighting tactics to make me feel guilty and crazy for even suggesting he would do such a thing, qualities notorious of narcissists that back in the day I had no awareness of, other than the Red Flags that popped up now and again indicating something was amiss. I often dismissed these warnings, believing it was me being untrusting, which was a no-no in my repertoire at the time. Now I was confident that Lloyd was lying, and I told him so. Without further effort on my part, he fessed up.

The strong sense of knowing that reverberated throughout my body wasn't enough to ward off the shock, which suggests an adage often referenced with romance. *Love is blind.* We tell ourselves lies to avoid the pain that comes with discovering the truth that someone we loved and trusted has betrayed us.

Love has turned many of us into starry-eyed believers that negate what we don't want to know. I was heartbroken.

I sent Lloyd packing, but that didn't prevent the predictable trajectory of my future relationships. Back then I focused on the *right* guy or the *right* relationship instead of the Red Flags that offered me guidance; hence, three divorces to come, bouts of job dissatisfaction, and strained family relationships.

I remained unaware of this pattern for years, another Red Flag to contend with. It was me who doubted me and the guidance I was receiving. I became an avid People Pleaser and enabled much of the drama that entered my life. When you don't trust yourself, you look to others to define you. Red Flag!

Standing in my kitchen decades later, I knew there were more lies with Lloyd, countless warnings informing me things were shady all those years ago; the exes that would call when I visited, the day he broke up with a girlfriend on the phone in front of me moments after we vowed to be exclusive. Then there were times he made excuses for canceling a weekend last-minute, professing he had to study. It was crystal clear that Red Flags appeared way before and after my relationship with Lloyd, and that they would continue to show up because they are meant to.

From this moment on, I vowed to welcome and embrace Red Flags as the supportive guidance that they are, and to allow them to influence my choice-making process, especially if they steer me away from an outcome I desire. This is what clear guidance is. It isn't about getting what we want, it's about what is in our best interest to have. We must be open to receiving this valuable information so we can make the right choices for us.

Embarking on this endeavor of masterminding a book about Red Flags and their purpose not only became my priority, but my mission to live differently, in hopes that by publishing this book, others would follow suit and see Red Flags as the greatest advisors for their life.

If we want to live our best life as we intend, we must consider every choice we make and follow the best guidance we're given. Red Flags will show us the way because warnings are meant to get our attention. It's the offenses that support us in examining our worth and it's the darkness that will lead us through to the light if we are willing to see the truth.

As I put words down on paper, I wondered what vital information I would share about Red Flags other than the obvious *warning signs* they signify, how we often *turn away* from them and the *effect they have* when we do, but in time I felt confident that I would know, and before long, I possessed a wealth of insights that got me stoked to get this book out into the world.

I contacted my publisher last fall and signed a contract for launching in late summer. I took a deep, cleansing breath and cultivated faith that this would be my best book to date and perhaps my final one. I like to end on a high note.

Each time I commit to such an undertaking, I know that I too will be put through an initiation of sorts, where I am physically, emotionally and mentally tested by the subject matter I am writing about. I expected a bumpy ride and a cathartic experience. I was spot on.

Once my manuscript was complete with all expectations met, it was ready for the publication process. My anticipation of getting this book in your hands became a reality and I celebrated a newfound gratitude for my future too. I firmly believe that we are being guided 24/7, and if we are willing to follow our inner voice, we will live the life we intend.

When Red Flags appear these days, I welcome them with curiosity and fascination instead of fear and doubt. Implementing the Essential Rules daily has made my life magical. I no longer second-guess myself and I am making choices with clarity and ease. I hope this will be for you too.

CHOICES

CHOICES

Whether you know it or not, believe in it or not, or give it much thought, every choice you make has cumulatively brought you to where you are today. In the same way, every choice you make from this moment on will take you to where you will be tomorrow. Your choices make up the pinnacle of your life.

Every choice we make affects our self-worth, our relationships with others, adds or depletes the meaning we give to our lives, and has everything to do with the experiences we have. There isn't anything more important than the choices we have made, the ones we make now, and those we will make in the future.

Doesn't it pay, then, to have a strategy for making the best choices possible? Doesn't it make sense to have a support structure to count on? My intention for creating this book is precisely this: to provide Essential Rules for guiding your choices. Stay tuned.

It's important to understand the impact of our choices and how we reach our conclusions. Rules for reference will steer us to the right path, just as Red Flags that vie for our attention are designed to do; however, we may choose to negate this guidance and decide differently, leading us astray.

I am a firm believer that despite our claims for the truth, we yearn for the fantasy or illusion we have created, the vision in our mind's eye of a life we believe will bring us happiness, meaning and purpose.

Whether it's the *should* life, the fairy tales we grew up with, or that which we believe will bring the experiences we want, our dreams hold the power to override any truth we profess to want to know. Even when it's evident we are lying to ourselves, our desire to keep the illusion alive will keep the truth at bay.

When we resist facing the pain of our circumstances, we cling on tightly to our rationalizations, justifications, and excuses to explain why we make the choices we make. Our dreams can manipulate our choices, just as much as they do with fear of not getting what we want or losing what we have. So, the Red Flags that interfere with this process become unwelcome visitors. We pretend we don't see them or find ways to explain them away. Soon we forget they were there. But they never leave us. I'll delve into this further in the section on Red Flags.

There may be times when our choice aligns with our inner guidance and leans toward trusting a Red Flag for the warning it brings, to then hear the opinions and advice of others who encourage us to trust, to give second chances, and tell us we're too picky or inflexible. So, we step over our truth and make choices based on what others think and feel. This brings about confusion, discomfort, and much rumination, making the decision process more frustrating in the future because we question our feelings and second-guess them. Soon, we lose trust in our perception of things. This is where we falter.

If we wake up to this destructive pattern that is preventing us from the happy life we desire, we can shift gears and follow the guidance the Red Flags are cautioning us to heed. Then, we will embark on the very path that will take us to our intended life. Our built-in guidance system exists to support us on our journey, and all that's needed is to have faith in the process. Red Flags prompt us to stop, beware, listen, trust the warning, and follow its direction.

It makes sense that if we are warned about something, that we are being directed toward another course of action, a different choice. At the very least, Red Flags are asking us to examine and evaluate a situation that raises concern, and to take it seriously.

So often, though, we spend time spinning in circles, confused and distressed, claiming we don't know what's the best choice to make. And if you examine your past closely, you may reach the shocking conclusion that many of the choices you made may not have been your own. Instead, the opinions and influences of others you gave credence to either by admiring them or fearing them have taken precedence.

Since everyone is privy to the *Should* life or the *Right Way* of doing things by what we've been conditioned to believe, it makes sense choosing to live in ways that are expected of us can result in becoming unaligned with who we are and what we desire. This is a tragedy.

And this is a biggie. *Drum roll please...*

If we believe others as they profess themselves to be, without addressing our suspicions or concerns about their propositions, our choices can hit the ground running to join on to whatever charade is being presented, especially when we're hearing what we've always hoped for. It's another strong example of how powerful our fantasies are and how they pull the wool over our eyes. Narcissists and conmen are masters at knowing what we want and then selling it to us.

And guess what?

Most of the time many of us don't realize we're making choices that aren't ours. We are knee-deep in our patterns that dictate our actions. This is why I believe many people struggle with decisions. They aren't aware of what they want and need because they are focused on everyone else. It's downright aggravating!

Then, there are those who sense at some point they are stepping over themselves, people-pleasing, doing things they don't want to do, sucking it up, believing that someday it will pay off. They spend much of their time convincing themselves that these choices that don't feel good, that don't align with who they are and what they want, are somehow their choice. Many people stuck in this pattern claim to feel crazy.

Our truth remains hidden because admitting self-betrayal is a shameful and painful reality for many to swallow. At some point, it becomes evident when faced with the dreaded question:

"Is this all there is?"

This is when people reach out to a professional for support. We wait until it feels as if there's nowhere to turn to. This is a fertile time for growth and healing.

There is no doubt in my mind that when we are unaligned with our truth and our heart's desire to live the life we intend, we will experience discomfort, a lack of joy, disillusionment, and depression.

It won't matter if we are living a privileged life where our basic needs are being met, and we don't have to struggle to make ends meet. There are many people who are miserable when they have much to be grateful for. I am certain that living a life that is not intended causes a degree of malaise that takes over one's sense of being and overshadows all chances of getting to the truth.

Once we begin living a lie, we can bury it so deep that we don't even know we're doing it; hence, the well-known acronym for denial: "**D**idn't **E**ven **N**otice **I** **A**m **L**ying." When the truth doesn't see the light of day, it can send people to their graves deceiving themselves.

As an Emotional Wellness Coach supporting clients to step into their lives with both feet, and heal what ails them, I hear all sorts of stories, and many are heartbreaking. I, too, have not been immune to self-worth issues and struggles in life, not to mention bad decision-making. As an avid People Pleaser for decades, I was making choices based on *them*, whoever *they* were at the time. There were many Red Flags that went unheeded.

Years ago, I received a call from Joanne, who was desperate to help her sister get out of a toxic relationship. Joanne was concerned and adamant that coaching was a last-ditch attempt to get Melissa to see the situation clearly. She offered to cover the coaching fee.

"Melissa needs to leave her cheating husband before they decide to have a family," Joanne insisted.

During the three months I supported Melissa, I was concerned for her too. There were many Red Flags about her relationship that struck me. Melissa was aware of them too. When I asked her about the advice she would give to a good friend in the same predicament, she said without hesitation that she would tell her friend to leave the relationship.

As a Coach, with the intention of encouraging my clients to follow their heart, I do not steer them in any direction, other than to explain all options and the importance of choosing with clarity. The coaching sessions are designed to support my clients to connect with their inner wisdom for answers and guidance. This is pertinent to support making choices that are right for them.

I empower my clients to take responsibility for co-creating all their relationships and urge them to put weight on the choices they make, especially if they choose out of fear and go against their gut instincts. Fear can be a big motivator for staying complacent even when it doesn't feel good, especially when we don't have faith in ourselves or our future, believing we can't make it on our own.

Even though it's impossible to know the outcome of things, it is very possible to predict how things may turn out. Red Flags are essential guidance because warnings are indicators urging us away from something. If we pay attention to the signs, we can change our course and make a different choice.

But despite the guidance we are given, and the choice we make to ignore our cautionary advisors, I am a firm believer that we make the *right* choice at the *right* time for the *right* reasons based on who we are at the time and the lessons we need to learn to grow and evolve.

As our sessions neared their conclusion, it was evident that in Melissa's past, she was making everyone else's choices but her own. And even though our work together supported her immensely, she agreed to coaching to appease her sister Joanne. It was evident to me that Melissa was yearning for autonomy, and to make her own decisions, even when she felt she was taking a risk that may backfire causing her a lot of pain. Sometimes, making *our* choice is enough to be the *right* choice, regardless of the Red Flags warning us otherwise. Melissa chose to stay in her relationship.

Lastly, the more we make choices based on other people's opinions and turn away from the Red Flags that are vying for our attention, we will not only lose trust in ourselves, but we will also begin to raise some Red Flags for others to experience with us. Stay tuned.

RED FLAGS

RED FLAGS

A nudge from our gut. An uneasy feeling. A hunch something is off. A warning. An alert to danger. The Red Flags that vie for our attention urging us to heed them.

Red Flags show up randomly, unexpectedly, and sometimes predictably. They have the power to burst our bubble amid any joyful experience we're in the middle of, dropping our mood within seconds to that of concern.

They may surprise us, or even shock us, leaving the impression that we've been blindsided by events we couldn't foresee. And even when we predict them, we may choose to discount or ignore them with a brush off the shoulder, or rationalizations that we're overthinking things.

But no matter how Red Flags reach our awareness, they show up steadily in our search for meaning. They are all around us, or better stated in a favorite Beatles love song: *Here, There and Everywhere.*

I can't think of a place where Red Flags don't show up. Whether politically, professionally, socially, or within religious organizations; they exist with family, friends, co-workers, and acquaintances. They are present in all our relationships, including the connection we have with ourselves. And unless you live under a rock, a big Red Flag, you've been privy to these warnings.

A big intention of mine is to encourage you to see this cautionary guidance as an essential part of the support you are gifted with, to welcome it, and to follow it. I believe Red Flags are the soundest, clearest advice we have for guiding our choices. After all, haven't we prayed to be shown the way? Perhaps being cautioned *away* from something is the way.

Red Flags are the answer to our prayers because, even though we recognize them outside of ourselves, the cues come from within us, from the knowledge we possess, the lessons we've learned and the way we've been conditioned to believe in right and wrong, good and bad.

And even though it may appear that our gut and intuition may be separate from the warnings we notice outside of us, I believe our gut and intuition play a huge part in the way we sense things, process them, and act on them. So, where many profess there's a distinct difference, including Google, I believe we each see Red Flags based on our own unique ability to read a room, assess people's intentions, and trust the information that comes from within.

Red Flags inform us of something that needs our attention, particulars that are important and pertinent for us to know about our relationships and the choices we make. They can also spark our attention to the familiarity they convey with situations in the past that were hurtful. They alert us to pause, evaluate, and raise questions.

The term, *cold feet*, which many of us see as a natural state of being when making a big investment or a life-long decision such as marriage, seems normal and expected. It's the Red Flag many of us explain away with the phrase: *oh, it's just cold feet, it happens to everyone*. But I wonder whether nerves that rise when we're about to take a leap have everything to do with the Red Flags we've ignored, now conducting a choir of urgency as we're about to jump.

I feel certain that the warnings we have seen cannot be unseen and become warehoused within our psyche. Whether we like it or not, this information lives within us and will come up now and again, most likely at the most inopportune times or when we're close to making a choice that's not in our best interest. Either way, they exist for us, not against us. They are here to guide us.

Imagine being a juror in a murder case, when the prosecutor, a smart one, makes an inference that the defendant's alibi is shady and impossible to prove, to create doubt in the jurors' minds. The defense attorney abruptly objects, the judge sustains and demands the comment be stricken from the record. The jury is instructed to ignore what they heard and prohibited from using the information in their deliberation.

Despite following the judge's instructions, I don't need to spell it out. What's heard cannot be unheard. Even if you as a juror comply with the law, you have information that may sway your decision.

Since Red Flags cannot be unseen or forgotten, despite our ignoring them, it can feel as if they haunt us with their cautionary energy, especially when we continue to rationalize them away. But not heeding a Red Flag for information won't make it nonexistent. They have their effect whether we acknowledge them or not. Our subconscious is very powerful, and Red Flags are very much alive here.

When a Red Flag shows up, it's noticed. Each time we turn away, we unlock another lie we tell ourselves, and that process can either happen consciously or unconsciously. The more we deceive ourselves, the greater the likelihood we fall into a pattern that lands us on shaky ground, wondering how we got there.

Feeling blindsided can happen to the most rational people who believe they never saw *it* coming, even though they were warned more than once. We blame others for our reality when we misplace our faith in *them*, instead of the guidance we are given, and thus avoid taking responsibility for stepping over the Red Flags, hoping for the outcome we want.

Back in 2007, I traveled from my then home, New York City, New York, to San Diego, California, for a three-day intensive workshop that was mandatory I attend to earn my Life Coach certification.

Having been to several of these workshops before, I was privy to the strict protocol. Cell phones are to remain off other than one call per day in case of emergency or to check on children; otherwise, it's recommended to refrain from connecting with the outside world. When the long day concludes, much of the evening is spent doing assigned homework that is due the following morning.

On the second night of my trip, I found myself reeling from an incident I didn't expect. It sent me into a tailspin; its effect unleashing a series of lies I would tell myself. Even now as I write this, admitting my surprise at the time, I know that I was censoring my feelings to cover up what I didn't want to know.

A few months before the trip, I met Matt on a dating site. After some messages back and forth, and a lengthy chat on the phone, we set up a lunch date at a popular New York City restaurant the following week.

I arrived first and was seated at a small table for two near the window. A few minutes later I spotted Matt coming through the door. I recognized him from his profile photos thinking it a plus, since many people on these sites include outdated pictures that look nothing like they do here and now.

We connected instantly. The smile we exchanged spoke volumes of approval and I found Matt very funny and engaging, qualities I found attractive, hence, my *type* of guy. I was excited.

One Red Flag that stood out for me was how Matt volunteered to taste my food and wasn't the slightest bit shy about it. I always found it interesting how some people feel comfortable to help themselves with what they want. I found it gutsy, since I judged myself as someone who wouldn't do that and wondered whether it was me who should be more assertive. I brushed it off with the excuse that I was being too picky.

Since I was excited and eager to start a new relationship a few years after my marriage ended, I was pushing for Matt to be that guy. So, when he phoned me not too long after our first date asking me out on a few dates, one in which his family would be present, I felt a surge of suspicion, (Red Flag). *It's way too soon. (Red Flag.) It's way too fast. (Red Flag.)* But instead, I stuck my hand deep inside my bag of excuses and chalked it down to me being unaccustomed to being adored by a guy that's smitten.

As my trip to San Diego neared, Matt and I grew close. It had only been a couple of months, but moving at a fast pace made it seem like we knew each other for years. And even though we only spent the weekends together, since we lived a good distance away and worked long hours during the week, we spoke on the phone daily and I felt confident things were headed in a good direction.

Before boarding the plane, I explained the workshop protocol to Matt and asked him not to call me. I made sure to let him know that any distractions could interfere with my experience and hinder my process. I thanked him for understanding and told him that I would get in touch on my way home and that I would miss him very much.

The second night of the workshop I went to my room after dinner to pick up a notebook. While I was there, I turned on my phone to make sure I received a three-word text that I requested daily from my dog sitter, *all is well*, so I could relax knowing my fur babies were fine. As my phone lit up, I was surprised to see a voicemail from Matt and wondered what could be wrong, so I listened to it.

"I know you told me not to call, but I really miss you and very much want to hear your voice. I hope you call me back."

It hit me like a brick. That familiar sense of dread that permeated throughout my body whenever I felt triggered. An involuntary physiological sensation that I couldn't stop or contain. I began shaking as the familiar rant of the past played out in my mind. *You don't count, you're unimportant, who cares what you ask, it's not about you, no one respects you, no one takes you seriously.*

After some deep breathing, I texted Matt, thanked him for his call, indicated that I missed him too, and would call from the airport on my way home in a couple of days. I was angry at myself for responding but felt very uncomfortable doing nothing. I didn't want to make him feel bad, even though I was disappointed. I pretended to be grateful. (Red Flag.) It made me feel worse.

The following morning at breakfast, a workshop attendee asked if I was feeling well. I confided in her about Matt's call and how I felt disrespected. She encouraged me to embrace it, that he just missed me, that I was lucky and that she hopes she'll find a nice guy like Matt. I was surprised at her response, and believed she meant well and was trying to cheer me up, but I couldn't help but feel slighted yet again. My feelings didn't seem to matter.

Even so, I made the choice to consider her advice and rationalize away my concerns into becoming more grateful. This was a major pattern in my life for a very long time as an avid People Pleaser. Listening to what others felt and going along with the consensus. (Red Flag). I will discuss more about this pattern when I present the Essential Rules.

Fast forward two shaky years, with more than one breakup under our belts, Matt and I got married and subsequently divorced five years into our union. We went our separate ways and never spoke again.

The Red Flag that warned me years ago, the unwanted phone call on my trip to San Diego and the unsettling feeling it sparked, set the tone and theme for our relationship. Red Flags would follow, painting a clear picture for what's to come. Matt was a Narcissist, and I was a People Pleaser and Enabler. A perfect match for a toxic relationship.

I mentioned earlier about challenging the expression that *Hindsight is 20/20*.

Even though it makes sense to believe it's easier to see things more clearly, connecting events to an outcome once they have been reached, I am going to suggest that it's another excuse we use to deflect taking responsibility for neglecting the Red Flags that vie for our attention. For many of us, taking responsibility is painful and shameful. It's easier to blame others or claim we didn't see it coming, than to admit we screwed up.

And, for those who claim they were blindsided, innocent to warning signs along the way, may instead deny or refute them, without knowing they are doing this. We protect ourselves in situations we fear or believe we cannot handle.

To further challenge *Hindsight is 20/20*, we don't need an outcome to predict the accuracy of Red Flags. While there are several scenarios that can result from a warning, none of which is certain, we only need to know there's information and guidance to follow. A warning is a warning. Period.

Did you ever get strong feelings you couldn't ignore?

You were about to make a choice with ease at one moment, to find in the next a strong nudge urging you to rethink your decision. Rationalize and justify as you may, you can't shake the feeling, so you make a different choice, speculating something bad may happen, even when you have no evidence to back it up. If you choose to step over the feeling, the anxiety can be overwhelming. Personally, when these strong gut feelings happen, I listen to them, and believe I dodged a bullet.

Even though Red Flags and gut feelings can appear as if they are separate and different, Red Flags typically noticed through people's behavior, boundaries being crossed, things appearing off, or obvious danger signs, I believe strongly that there is a strong connection because gut feelings often come from lessons we've learned, knowledge we have or past dangers we've been conditioned to believe are pertinent to beware of; e.g., *don't talk to strangers*.

And I also believe that intuitively we possess information that doesn't need an outside stimulus to ignite a strong feeling about someone or something. It's as if we can detect the Red Flags before they appear. I believe we have a built-in Red Flag alert system that we can count on to direct us toward safety.

Some who have rationalized this guidance later admit that the feeling was so profound, they question why they didn't follow it, reprimanding themselves for being careless and irresponsible for what might have happened. And sadly, for others, making a different choice led to a negative experience that brought with it much suffering. We must be willing to acknowledge the warnings we are given and to heed them.

One event that sits at the front of my mind explains this phenomenon to me, since many times I have no evidence of what was prevented by following its direction. I can only speculate. But this experience solidified any questions I had, and I became a believer. And because I was spared from being traumatized for life, I am grateful for these warnings and for heeding them.

In 2018, my mother lived in the memory care unit at a facility twenty minutes away from my home. She recently had surgery on her leg and was recovering nicely. Her follow-up doctor's appointment was scheduled for later in the week, Friday morning, September 7th at 10:00 a.m. Her private aide offered to take her.

The night before my mother's appointment, I felt anxiety about not being with her at the doctor's office. After all, I take copious notes, know the right questions to ask, and she appreciates me being there. But I reminded myself how overwhelmed I was with work, overseeing my mother's care, and wanting some ME time for a social life. I would have to change my day around, cancel lunch with a friend, and reschedule an appointment. I decided to leave things as they were and went to sleep.

The next morning, I rose early, fed my dogs, and slipped on my sneakers to take them for a walk, when the rumination began again. *I should be there for my mother.* I felt guilty and torn between supporting my mother vs. honoring some ME time. Being a People Pleaser, it was a well-oiled pattern of mine to prioritize others.

As I walked my dogs I was preoccupied with a potpourri of thoughts. *You should be there. No one listens as intently as you do. You can ask the doctor questions. Your mother would love you to be there. Go. You should go.*

Then a chorus rang out in my mind that drowned out the previous thoughts. *Don't be so controlling and anxious. Your mother is going to be fine. You say you want to delegate more, so delegate. Your mother's aide is more than capable of handling this; she's a professional, you're not.*

Whoa. My mind was reeling from all the chatter.

Then, I became distracted when my puppy, Priscilla, vomited a few times along our walk. This was unusual and now there was only one decision to consider. Cancel my day and get Priscilla to the vet.

When I returned home from our walk, I was in the process of texting my friend to cancel lunch, when a loud voice in my head insisted on waiting.

"Priscilla will be fine. Wait ten minutes."

Shortly after, Priscilla became playful, and her eyes looked bright. I told myself to get it together and relax. I assured myself that everything would go well and I would see my mother later that afternoon and get an update on her doctor's visit then. I was now ready to start my day worry free.

Linda was seated when I arrived for lunch at noon. I apologized for keeping my phone out in case the aide needed to get in touch with me. Two hours passed since my mother's scheduled appointment time, so I suspected she may be headed back to the facility by now.

Linda and I chatted about what was new in our lives, when suddenly, I felt ill. A wave of nausea came over me and my stomach felt sour. I excused myself and headed for the bathroom. When I returned, Linda noticed I wasn't looking well and asked if there was anything she could do.

"I don't know what I can eat. My stomach feels queasy, and I feel a headache coming on."

But I insisted on staying, took something for my headache and soon I felt better. We spent a couple of hours together and then parted ways.

I headed to the facility to visit my mother. When I arrived, I couldn't find her. She wasn't in her room or the living room, and when I spotted a staff member and inquired, I was told that my mother was at a doctor's appointment.

"The appointment was at 10:00 a.m., it's now 2:20 p.m.," I told the staff member.

"Her appointment was at 1:00 p.m." she responded.

Gosh, I thought. *How could I mix up those times? I am positive I was told the appointment was at 10:00 a.m.*

Feeling crazy, I went back to my car and planned to go home, telling myself I would see my mother the next morning. I glanced at my phone and noticed a voice message from my mother's aide.

"Your mother wasn't breathing well at the doctor's office, so we are on the way to the hospital."

I drove quickly and my heart was pounding. The hospital was only five minutes away from the facility and as I turned onto the street that leads to the emergency room, my phone rang. It was my sister, and she was crying. I could hardly make out what she was saying when her crying escalated, and she said it again.

"Mommy died."

"No! Wait. What?"

I was devastated. I had no words. No thoughts. I felt as if I was wrapped in a blanket of surreal nothingness walking through a dense fog.

I was directed to the area in the emergency room of the hospital where my mother was taken. The curtain was drawn. I announced myself and the voice inside asked me to wait.

"Let me in!" I demanded. "Please let me in. I am her daughter."

My mother had passed only moments before. Her body was warm, and her eyes were open. She looked scared. I held her hand and cried.

To this day, I replay the events that happened the night before, and morning of the day my mother left the physical world, September 7, 2018. She was ninety and a half years old.

Her aide, who was noticeably shaken and upset, shared that it was sudden. My mother became sick at the doctor's office, she couldn't breathe well, and they drove to the Emergency Room as fast as they could. There were attempts to revive my mother, but she was gone.

There is no doubt in my mind that I was being guided away from witnessing my mother's death. I also feel certain that the sudden illness I felt at lunch either preceded or coincided with my mother becoming unwell at the doctor. Even though I felt guilty that I wasn't by her side, I knew in my heart that I would be traumatized for life had I been there. I was grateful that I was spared.

A few nights later, I picked up the book, *The Tibetan Book of Living and Dying*, and turned to a random page. It stated that people at the time of death prefer to be alone because it's easier to leave without their loved ones surrounding them, which makes it more difficult for them to let go. This brought me peace.

There were a couple of stories told by relatives who claimed to be by their dying loved one's bedside for hours to leave for a short bathroom trip or to get a cup of coffee, to learn upon returning of their loved one's passing.

It makes me wonder whether the strong impulses we get are related to Red Flags being delivered energetically and telepathically, as well as intuitively, and whether people with heightened intuitions are privier to the premonitions they experience.

On September 10, 2001, I returned to my New York City home from a trip to eastern Europe. It was 6:00 p.m. when the plane landed and I arrived at my Upper East Side apartment by 7:30 p.m. I ate a light dinner and went straight to bed. I was exhausted.

That night I slept deeply and had a strange, vivid dream. A large commercial plane was headed toward my fifteenth story window. Just before the nose of the plane hit the glass, I abruptly woke in a pool of sweat, my heart was pounding, and I had a hard time getting back to sleep.

My phone rang the next morning. I glanced at the clock and realized I had overslept. As I picked up the phone I could hear the urgency in my mother's voice, insisting I turn on the news. I was shocked and horrified as I watched the planes crashing into the World Trade Center, exploding on impact. The terrorist attacks that shocked New York and the world on Tuesday, September 11, 2001 was a tragedy that changed the world forever.

It was a warm, sunny morning and it felt surreal to have arrived home from eastern Europe less than twenty-four hours before the attacks, and to be physically a subway ride away from the sheer devastation and the many lost lives. I didn't connect until later that I knew some of the people who perished. And I still wonder whether my dream, with its foreboding nature, foretold what was to come.

More familiar ways we spot Red Flags are in our day-to-day lives, interacting with others, when we're alerted to something that stands out or seems off. Whether it's a boundary being crossed, hearing an inconsistent explanation that spells lying, or having a strong hunch that our partner's phone holds some secrets we may want to know.

Whenever we feel suspicious, there will be a Red Flag to vouch for. And regardless of the way they show up, they are here to support us, to direct us, and to warn us. We must be willing to heed them.

It is important to mention though, that being suspicious when alerted that something is off vs. expecting things to go wrong are two very different experiences with two very different outcomes. There's a difference between turning away from a Red Flag and seeking out Red Flags where there may be none. Looking for Red Flags vs. allowing Red Flags to alert you are two very different ways of living and relating in relationships.

When we turn away from Red Flags, they get stored within our psyche. They don't fade, and they won't disappear.

Red Flags, when unacknowledged and unheeded, gain power over our mindset because once we see them, we become sensitized to them. If we attempt to ignore them, our suspicions get filtered in with our judgments which influence how we think and what we believe. This adds confusion to our choice-making.

Once self-doubt sets in, we second-guess ourselves, and each time we turn away from our guidance, we become guarded and expect that others will disappoint us, even before any evidence presents itself to prove we're right. Before long, we slip into a pattern where we manipulate our experiences instead of allowing them to unfold organically and to evolve toward healthy connections. Our relationships become strained.

Without thinking, we seek out Red Flags anywhere and everywhere with everyone because we now have knowledge they exist, and we expect we'll see them again with others.

Isn't this good enough reason to heed the Red Flags?

Toxic relationships manifest when we attract situations and circumstances into our lives to bring resolution and closure to past upsets, going all the way back to early childhood. Red Flags are the guidance to steer us toward harmony because being warned away from danger is the *right* direction to turn. But we get in the way of this process.

We've been conditioned to be positive, to trust others, to see the good in all, to discard the individual for the collective, when the best guidance we're given remains *under wraps*. Our rationalizations and justifications take precedence over the messages that would behoove us to heed, so that we can make the appropriate choices that serve us. Instead, we manipulate our circumstances to achieve whatever outcome we desire even when all evidence proves we've veered off course some time ago.

Another way we sabotage ourselves is by judging ourselves for having judgments, especially the negative kind. And many people attach negative judgments to Red Flags. I believe this is the biggest impediment to why we avoid guidance.

Red Flags carry a dark energy that many people believe is wrong to consider. The efforts we put forth to be positive, to do for others, be there for others, be better for others, and make others come first, carries more weight than any suspicions we may have. Instead, we give second chances, benefit of the doubt, and lots of free passes to avoid being seen as impatient, inflexible, intolerant or, heaven forbid, *selfish*.

Even the phrase, *self-care isn't selfish*, is touted so often to make others feel at ease about attending to themselves because deep down we've been taught and conditioned to believe that making ourselves the priority is *selfish*, and no one wants to be *that*. Many people who suffer from insecurities and feel not good enough continue to strive to be better, not for themselves, but for others. The self gets left out and all relationships suffer as a result.

Imagine that every quality has a positive or negative charge. If you choose to exude a quality, you can regulate it, add grace to it, amp it up, tone it down. But anything you don't want to be and hide from being will likely exaggerate your expression and embarrass you.

I am happy to sit down with anyone at any time and debate that we are all selfish, all of us, all of the time. No one does something without getting something back. Even those who aim to be selfless do it for the feeling it brings. All humans with an ego are self-absorbed; otherwise, we wouldn't be able to make sense of our experiences.

Whereas it's great to look at the bright side of things, keep an upbeat attitude and believe in the benevolence of others, we must accept that there are people who aren't interested in our best interests. Warnings are as valuable as being directed toward buried treasure because we must accept that there are wrongdoers and evil in the world and that we need to protect ourselves. I believe many people feel it's selfish and untrusting to be guarded and so they put others first and step over their guidance.

Does this make any real sense to you?

The timing of this book is a perfect example of how we ignore our guidance and comply with the agenda of others, even if it makes no sense. When it comes to authority, we're taught and conditioned to trust, so we comply instead of exercising our curiosity.

How many Red Flags have you spotted during 2020 - 2025?

I won't belabor my point, but it makes sense to look back and count the Red Flags along the way. I must admit that I lost a lot of faith in humanity, authority, regulatory agencies, the medical industry, and especially the media.

You can be the judge for yourself of what didn't feel right to you and what you are willing to accept and believe. But for me, when things don't add up, I get curious, suspicious and want answers to my questions. There's a lot of shady shenanigans going on in the world that make no sense.

Red Flags often arrive as deflections. Phrases designed to skip over or change a subject: "That's anecdotal." "That's misinformation." "It's a conspiracy theory." "That's not based in fact." Deflections in and of themselves are Red Flags because they aim to steer us away from knowing something that we're curious about or have confusion around. Ask a question, get brushed off with a one-liner, and you will detect the shady nature and spot the Red Flag.

If your husband comes home with lipstick on his collar, spends hours in the bathroom whispering on his phone, or comes home late from work way too often, you may have suspicions. Ask a question and get brushed off with "It's nothing." "I'm not whispering." "It was work." "What lipstick?" "Oh that, I bumped into Lucy in the coffee room, it must have rubbed off. Damn, do you think the stain will come out?" These statements brush off, deflect or gaslight, implying there's nothing to be suspicious about and even suggest that it's you who is crazy, paranoid, suspicious, and untrusting.

Frustration gets thrown into the mix when we accept these deflections instead of investigating and seeking the truth. Some keep their blinders fixed to maintain the illusion of the outcome they want or remain deluded by what they assure themselves would never happen. Thus, the Red Flags get pushed aside, or so they think.

Each one of us has values, beliefs and passions. We experience all sorts of moods and feelings that we must honor. We must stop doubting ourselves and own our perspective on things instead of relying on others to make sense about how we see things.

Listen closely to your family, friends, and partners, and notice how they do this too. They censor what they say, apologize if they cry, and make inferences to what they should and shouldn't do. When we do this, it doesn't serve anyone.

If we are willing to stop doubting our doubts, accept the judgments we have, both good and bad, without making any of them wrong, we will naturally allow the guidance that comes to us and from us, based on what feels *right to us*. We will learn to trust ourselves and claim our rights as human beings to express who we are.

The expression, *rejection is direction,* is one of my favorites because it supports having faith that we can't always know what's in our best interest. All that's needed is to examine our decision-making process and whether we struggle with making choices that support us. When we do not honor what we think and believe and instead make choices based on what others want or the consensus demands, we will likely make choices that are unaligned with who we are.

Doesn't it make sense then to heed the Red Flags?

Consider fear of failure. Why are so many of us remaining stagnant and motionless when it comes to following our dreams because we're afraid we will fail at something or disappoint someone?

How many Red Flags have you spotted while doing something you didn't love or agreed to do for someone because you couldn't say no?

If you ask me, I think the process of elimination is the best and surest way to achieve what we desire. It's the *make or break* that lets us know if we are in the right place doing what feeds our soul vs. living the should life or choosing for *them*. Red Flags are our best friends when it comes to determining whether we are on the right path for us, living the life we intend.

How do we move toward something new if we believe moving on means we've failed at something and are seen as a quitter and a loser?

Once we embrace that the process of elimination is our surest path to finding what we love and to embrace it instead of making it wrong, we will be led to that which makes our heart sing. And Red Flags are our trusty friends that make sure we're informed when it's time to make the move.

NEXT!

If I haven't listed enough perks for heeding Red Flags, allow me to introduce one that's a doozy when it comes to doubting whether to follow the warnings of Red Flags, to process them and to follow their guidance.

For each Red Flag we ignore, we raise at least five Red Flags for others to see with us. Red Flags unaddressed affect our behavior and will expose our suspicious nature by the qualities we exude. Whereas we were once approachable, inviting and extroverted, we now appear overly guarded, untrustworthy, critical, shut down, closed off, paranoid and perhaps commitment phobic.

How fun would it be to live with someone who is looking for what's wrong?

My strong recommendation when it comes to Red Flags is to *allow* them to show themselves to you. Do not go on a scavenger hunt to seek them out. I am all for being protective and guarded, but if you approach everything with a suspicious nature that *nothing good will come from this*, that is what you will find. A healthy dose of curiosity is best, while keeping your antenna up for Red Flags to alert you.

One thing you can be sure of is that Red Flags are accurate, trustworthy, and loyal friends. And they will find you when the timing is right and they have information to share.

Red Flags may also appear when things are going so well, that they appear *too good to be true*. In these cases, you can be certain there's a Red Flag waving in the midst. Think about it. The phrase, *if it's too good to be true*, has suspicion written all over it. If we question a reality, especially if it's one we hope for, we should honor our concern. It's not that great things can't happen, but it's good practice to do our due diligence and follow our gut.

When I sold my apartment in New York City back in 2006, my boyfriend, Brian, offered me an opportunity to invest some of my newfound wealth, get a high interest return and make some *easy* money.

"I can help you grow your money and make a quick profit." Brian insisted that others were very pleased investing with him.

Even though Brian and I had recently become a couple, I knew him for a few years, and he had a good reputation. He explained the investment step by step and it made sense at the time. Brian complied with my request for a notarized promissory note that contained a clause for legal fees if things veered off course. We had a *meeting of minds* and Brian commended me for being responsible and protecting myself. I was eager to get started, even though it seemed *too good to be true.*

   I felt comfortable investing a small amount at first and gave Brian $1500. As promised, my money was returned on the last day of the following month plus ten percent. After some time, Brian encouraged me to increase the amount, and I agreed to $10,000, then $20,000. Once again, he came through and I was excited to make a few thousand dollars that would go towards paying the rent on my apartment.

   When it came time to make a new investment, I closed my eyes, said a prayer, and handed Brian $30,000. I must admit my anxiety was rising even though things had panned out so far. That Red Flag gnawing at my gut again, *this is too good to be true.* I assured myself Brian was trustworthy; but the suspicion remained, nonetheless.

   As the following month approached, Brian told me there was an issue returning my money on time. He said it would take a few more weeks and explained why. He assured me this wasn't unusual, sometimes delays happen, and told me not to be concerned. But once the new date arrived it was put off again and I freaked out. I suggested that Brian pay me with his own money and that he could wait. But he refused. I told him I didn't feel comfortable investing any more money with him.

To add fuel to the fire, we got into an argument unrelated to the money, and I made the decision to end the relationship. When Brian would not return my calls or respond to my emails regarding my investment, I thought I would never see that money. I had no idea who else I could contact. Brian was my only connection.

Red Flag Alert: never lend money you cannot afford to lose.

The chatter in my mind was endless. There it was again, that Red Flag, *this is too good to be true*, that I stepped over to make some extra money to instead lose a small fortune. It was now haunting me. But I refused to cower and back down.

I contacted an attorney, and we issued a Statutory Lien against Brian, which he confirmed receipt of in a frantic voicemail saying he couldn't lease an apartment because of the action I took against him. I must admit it felt euphoric to see him squirm, but I was still $30,000 out of pocket.

My attorney told me that Brian hired legal assistance, and they wanted to settle. Brian would pay me in installments for twelve months minus the interest I was paid in the other investments. I felt lucky to get any of that money back and agreed. I felt foolish that I bought into what I now knew was a Ponzi scheme.

At the end of one year, I was paid in full and received a profuse apology from Brian, which no longer had any credibility or meaning for me. Brian was a conman. The shining reputation others bestowed on him, turned out to be shady people themselves, with Red Flags I also ignored. I was mortified that Brian was a boyfriend who I once believed in, and who had betrayed my trust.

I suspect that many of Bernie Madoff's clients had questions and concerns too. I have no doubt there were Red Flags for many of them, even with a Ponzi scheme that was carried out for years. There's no way many of his clients missed the crimson cloth waving in their minds. *This is too good to be true.*

Many people spot Red Flags in their search for love and romance. We cannot always know whether a relationship will last, how things will pan out, whether we will be happy, or if someone may experience poor health or financial ruin. But if we are open to receiving guidance and allowing the Red Flags to inform us, we'll be ahead of the game in terms of predictability.

I met Daryl many years ago, when I lived in New York City. I had passed him on the street now and again and we exchanged smiles. So, when I saw him one evening walking home from work and he said hello and asked if we could chat for a moment, I was open. I found Daryl attractive and friendly. After we established that we were both single, he asked if I would like to have dinner sometime.

We began dating and, at my request, kept things at a slow, steady pace. We got together on Saturday evenings and I told Daryl, who asked me to get together during the week, that when my schedule with work lightened up, we would see each other more. It was an excuse on my part, as I had ended a relationship not too long ago and I wasn't ready.

A few months later, Daryl asked if he could spend the night at my apartment on a Thursday evening. He mentioned that he had a very early appointment in my neighborhood the following morning. I was conflicted but told myself to go ahead and give this relationship with Daryl a chance. I told him it would be fine, and I would make dinner.

Daryl arrived punctually at 6:00 p.m. He looked nice and I was excited to see him. He brought me beautiful flowers which I put in water and suggested he watch TV in the living room. I gave Daryl the heads up ten minutes before serving dinner. He smiled, turned off the TV, and went down the hall toward the bathroom and bedroom. About five minutes later, he came to the table in his underwear.

Take a deep breath. Have a chuckle. I couldn't believe it either.

Daryl was wearing his white Calvin Klein underwear and T-shirt. I was shocked, startled, baffled and lost for words. I had never been so turned off by someone so early in a relationship over what I thought was a major Red Flag.

"I see you've dressed for dinner."

Daryl detected the sarcasm in my voice and hurriedly turned for the bedroom to go and get dressed.

When he came back and sat down, he said he was sorry, but the look on his face spelled confusion.

"What's done is done. I just don't understand why you would do that." I looked at him inquisitively. Aside from being surprised, I sincerely wanted to know his thoughts. I was concerned about this new relationship that I had hopes for.

"I feel comfortable with you," Daryl said.

"I want you to feel comfortable with me, Daryl. But that's way too comfortable."

I told Daryl calmly and nicely that I felt disrespected. I reminded him that our relationship was new and even if it wasn't, I didn't appreciate what he did.

Daryl got very insulted and became belligerent. He raised his voice and told me that I was being critical and patronizing. It felt as if he was talking to someone else and directing his rant at me. I was becoming concerned about my safety and asked Daryl to leave. We didn't see each other again.

This incident was a blazing Red Flag for me for many reasons. It made Daryl appear lazy, way too comfortable, disrespectful, undemonstrative, inconsiderate, unromantic, immature; the list went on about the vision I had about where this relationship with Daryl would evolve.

But I must admit that I saw a big Red Flag with me as well. A pattern was emerging where I could see how I don't stand my ground and instead let others influence me to do things I don't want to do. I was a People Pleaser and had a hard time saying no. I talked myself into allowing Daryl over during the week when I wasn't ready. And the way the conversation escalated when I voiced my disapproval was a stark warning that I was dealing with a guy who had a temper.

Another Red Flag I regret stepping over happened two weeks before my wedding. I don't recall the incident that led to the huge argument with my fiancé Doug, only that I felt strongly that I shouldn't go ahead with the marriage. A loud thought reverberated in my head: *Don't marry that guy!* It was so strong it led to me having a conversation with my parents about it. They told me it was my decision and that if I wanted to call the marriage off I should.

But with the wedding so close, the arrangements all set, the people who were counting on me, the embarrassment I wanted to avoid and the hopeful dreamer I strived to be, I went ahead with the marriage, convincing myself that our love for each other would prevail. Despite my trepidation, and the Red Flags that warned danger, I believed things would work out. After eleven years, most of them unhappy, we divorced. I remarried twice after that, to two more narcissists and both unions ended in divorce as well.

News flash: It is possible, even probable, to love someone who isn't right for you. Red Flags will support seeing this truth if you allow them to inform you. I was a People Pleaser who attracted narcissistic men and had no clue I was dealing with a personality disorder. I know I had my own healing to do and that we cocreate all our relationships, but the Red Flags that vied for my attention went unheeded. I wasn't taking responsibility for my emotional wellness and for participating in toxic relationships.

I can say with certainty that my biggest regrets involve the ultimatum I gave to the three men I married. Personally, I feel strongly that ultimatums, in and of themselves and the energy they carry imply Red Flags, and I regret not heeding them.

Even though it may appear that someone complying with the fear of losing you can be seen as loving, it is eons away from someone proposing to you because they adore you and are excited to begin a life with you. Entering a union with excitement, love and faith is very different than stepping in with the fear of loss or commitment phobia. And just because people who fear marriage get married doesn't make them marriage material. Going ahead with anything out of fear is a Red Flag stepped over.

Even with my regrets, I don't dwell on them. I honor them as the choices I made at the time, understanding that all choices, both good and bad, are what help us grow, especially when we have no idea who we are. I know that it's likely nothing would change if I had to go back and do it over because we aren't privy to take our older, wiser self with us.

Based on who I was at the time, how I thought and what I believed in at that time, I made predictable choices. After all, if Red Flags and stepping over them has taught me anything, it's that my greatest Red Flag was that I didn't love myself and looked toward others to love and approve of me.

Another very important point to note about Red Flags and our willingness to acknowledge and heed them has to do with how deeply committed and invested we are in a relationship. I believe that the more interests we have, the harder it is to admit we're headed down a dark road.

I wasn't deeply invested in my relationship with Daryl, (the guy who wore his underwear to dinner), so it was easy for me to see the Red Flag in this relationship and end it quickly. But with Doug, my first husband, it was much more difficult. I went ahead with a marriage I had trepidation about because there were so many investments already in place.

If we love someone and hope to share a committed relationship with them, we are likely to step over the Red Flags we see because we desire a certain outcome. The phrase, *no one is perfect*, is a Red Flag expression we use to deflect a warning we'd rather not see. Even though it's true that each of us is flawed, I believe it's our investment we are trying to protect. Admitting that everyone has idiosyncrasies is a way we convince ourselves not to be concerned. Many times, we cling to a relationship in fear of losing something we don't even have.

When we hear about a stock market crash, it will have little direct effect on us, unless we have money invested in stocks. If our broker calms us down, assures us all will be well, that it's normal fluctuation in the market, we are likely to put the Red Flags that tell us otherwise at bay because the warnings go against the outcome we want, and we trust our financial advisor who had made us money in the past. We hold steady and pray he's right.

If we enter a business partnership with someone who is trustworthy and dependable, sign a contract, invest a lot of money and hire staff, we will likely rationalize and justify the Red Flags that pop up because we're both feet in and believe it's not easy to back out. So, hope keeps us believing everything will be okay.

When it comes to making sense of your choices and forgiving yourself for stepping over Red Flags, it's important to examine what your commitment and investment was at the time you made that choice. After all, we want to preserve and protect our greatest investments.

Going forward, I suggest and encourage you to consider your greatest interest and investment be your happiness and living your intended life. I have learned on my own journey that this is the path to victory.

The warnings we presently resist can lead us to higher ground if we are willing to follow their direction because we don't always know what is in our best interest, and I believe the Red Flags do.

It would be easy to fill more pages with Red Flag stories and examples, I have tons, but I have faith you have several of your own to refer to. My intention in writing this book is to support you to invite, allow, embrace and heed the Red Flags that come into your life, to welcome them as friendly visitors; not to fear them, discard them, step over them or ignore them. They are your guidance, and they are accurate.

How will you know?

Your gut knows! You will feel it! Trust it!

I have faith, as you read on, that past warnings you've stepped over will resurface. I suggest you buy a journal, preferably a red one, and take some notes about the Red Flags that show up because, after I present The Missed Guidance, The Unreachable Dream, and The Essential Rules for guiding your choices, you will be invited to an After Party. The After Party is a celebration and offers next steps once you've finished the book.

You will be invited to take a **Justice Journey** down **Red Flags Lane**, which will support you in seeing your experiences with new eyes. There will be instructions on how to write your **F**k You Declaration** that addresses anyone or anything that has stood or remains standing as an obstacle on your path to living your intended life. This will support releasing negative energy and moving forward with gratitude and attitude.

The After Party will support you in forgiving yourself, finding some closure and resolution for past hurts, and making peace with the guidance that went unheeded. There will also be a **spoonful of justice** stirred in.

So, let's get to the section on Missed Guidance to make sense of some of the nonsense that has us scratching our heads about why life doesn't show up the way we would like. To make peace with our past heartache, we must first understand how we search for meaning with the hopes of finding love.

THE MISSED GUIDANCE

Up to this point, I've covered the guidance we turn away from and the misguidance we follow. Both equally affect our choice-making, impacting all the experiences we have in life.

But there's another very important guidance that we are taught and conditioned to resist. And with all outside efforts steering us elsewhere, many, if not most of us comply.

I refer to this Missed Guidance as the *Game Changer* because it has the potential to deliver us our greatest life, one filled with love and appreciation for the self, while connecting with others in joyful, healthy ways. Ultimately, it's about discovering the deeper meaning of who we are and developing a greater understanding of our unique journey. There is no one exactly alike and there is no *One size fits all*, even though all misguidance suggests there is.

But before I present the Missed Guidance to you, it's crucial to explain why we've been complacent when it comes to considering going against the consensus and status quo. It's pertinent that I inform you why, with all our efforts, it appears fruitless in terms of gaining the love and respect we crave with the way we presently live. All the puzzle pieces must fit together to create the image with clarity.

Take a deep breath because this information may surprise and even offend you. You may close this book or throw it in the trash. And, if this is the case, I recommend you place it somewhere safe instead. Sooner or later, when you feel defeated, you may want to familiarize yourself with another approach to life; where you will not only get what you want and reap the benefits, you will have a different understanding of what it means to love your fellow man.

I live each day practicing this Missed Guidance and can vouch for its effectiveness. My hope is that you are open and willing to give it a try because once you become a master at it, you will celebrate and cultivate renewed hope for living the life of your dreams.

The Essential Rules, coming up soon, are designed so that you incorporate the Missed Guidance into your daily routine, to embrace the Red Flags as welcome visitors, and to ensure you live *your* intended life on *your* terms, while unburdening others so they can do the same for themselves.

There's an upside too for leaving our present teachings behind and embracing the Missed Guidance. After all, what we've been doing for eons has not been working. Just look at the state of the world. It was obvious to me the first time I became aware of the Missed Guidance. It not only made perfect sense, but it also offered an antidote for the disillusioned, lonely and lovelorn. And boy oh boy, as a People Pleaser for decades, I was stoked to jump on board.

The insanity of how we've been carrying on doing the same thing repeatedly with the same bad results is frustrating enough, but to expect we'll see anything different by amping up the same behavior, chanting the same message and singing the same song is outright crazy.

So here goes.

The way in which we live now, the guidance that steers us to resist the Missed Guidance, I refer to as the *Collective Red Flag*.

The *Collective Red Flag* hovers over us, ever so eloquently, influencing everything we think and do, despite not wanting to do many of the things we continue to do, are expected to do, and as of late, enforced to do.

What's the benefit of the *Collective Red Flag* you may wonder?

By now, if you've been a good person, it should be obvious. Everything we do is for the Greater Good, for the sake of *all* of us. The rationale being that we each eat, sleep, breathe and exist for everyone else. We strive to become our best selves so that together we prosper and prevail.

I must admit, such a life does sound wonderful. The perfect image of all of us around a campfire singing Kumbaya. Ah, what a dream. And I'm not being sarcastic. It would feel like nirvana. But this is not the reality which comes with following such guidance.

Not many spend their Saturday nights over dinner discussing the change we each personally must make. Instead, there's a plethora of pointing fingers at everyone else as the responsibility for what is. But I am certain many people think about it at night lying in bed, when solitude takes over and they have nowhere to go but within the recesses of their mind.

Like me, before I took it upon myself to embrace the Missed Guidance, they wonder whether they will ever have what they want, prosper more than just getting by, and feel inclusive when it comes to living in an abundant world and having the right to reap their share of the bounty. I can say that at this moment in time, more than most do not feel a part of any Greater Good, except for the elite whose bad idea it was in the first place and who praise its glory.

Despite many people feeling they're not good enough, believing life isn't fair and wondering when it's their turn to reap the rewards, most will not question this egregious system, because we are conditioned to believe that it will eventually pay off if we do our best to be better, not for ourselves, but for each other. Unfortunately, we're delivered blow after blow with the ongoing message that it's never enough despite what we do, and likely will never be.

Consider these questions:

If none of the parts count, what kind of sum does that make?

What is the benefit of a Greater Good when everyone feels unimportant, insignificant and left out?

What is the benefit of a Greater Good, or a Collective, when all the individuals that make up that sum are null and void?

Because whether you know it or not, or know it all too well, all of us have hidden questions and agendas where we consciously and unconsciously question: *Is this all there is? What about Me? What's in it for Moi?*

If the goal is for each of us to become the best we can be for *them*, the Collective, the Greater Good, whoever that really is, despite betraying *our* trust, sacrificing *our* integrity, livelihood, and even as of late, *our* health, with the insinuation that we be included in that *whole*, as long as we commit to excluding ourselves individually, let go of our independence and autonomy, and don't question the integrity of the agenda, how is it we benefit individually and how is it we benefit as a whole?

You may want to reread the last paragraph a few times to let it sink in. It's truly unbelievable that we buy into this sort of guidance. This makes no sense because nonsense has no worthy explanation.

You may disagree with me while others will cheer me on because if you're brutally honest, you will admit to the frustration and want answers to explain all the incompetence and corruption that's wreaking havoc in every corner of the world. People are disillusioned. Many are jobless and those who have jobs don't care to do them well.

It's a plethora of disrespect, inequality, and mostly a lack of desire to help each other out. I don't want to belabor the point, only to say we are doing things backwards and it isn't moving us forward.

So, the direction that behooves each of us to travel is to consider the opposite of what we are presently doing and get to the Missed Guidance, which is the guidance we are missing in our efforts to live a full, happy life, to prosper individually and to contribute to bettering the world.

There's one more caveat that's pertinent I preface: A big reason we've remained complacent, an obstacle so large it feels unimaginable to climb over, that so many continue to adhere to an agenda that hasn't been working, is because...drum roll please...

Most people would rather jump off a bridge than be labeled SELFISH!

OMG! I said it! The dirty word!

Consider this seriously for a moment and ask yourself this question:

What have you done in your life that you didn't want to do, so that you wouldn't be seen as selfish?

If I told you to make a list of one hundred things you've done that you didn't want to do, to avoid being seen as selfish, I have faith you would have that list in no time and even want to add a few hundred more you fell prey to.

So, before I lay out the plans for the Missed Guidance, allow me to inform you that everyone, even you, whether you like it or not, is **SELFISH!**

Every human being that has an ego is selfish because we must, despite aiming to be there for everyone else, be self-serving to make meaning of our lives and to survive. It's both a voluntary and involuntary process we cannot avoid, try as we may. But we can have control over who we are being and how we behave if we acknowledge and accept that we have choices about how we show up.

Like all qualities, *Selfish* has a negative and a positive expression. And we each embody both the dark and the light.

For each quality we accept and own as part of who we are, we can manage the expression of that quality because the moment we replace shame with compassion and stop making ourselves wrong for being *that* we become objective.

When we hide or avoid being a quality we don't want to be, just like most of us do with the selfish quality, these qualities take hold over us, and when we least expect it, they will show themselves in an exaggerated version that is likely to have others perceive us as amped up, overly reactive and even crazy. In the same way, not wanting to be selfish will make us appear overly selfish at some point in time, not just because we yearn to be all of who we are, but because we want what we want even when we're told we shouldn't want it. If we weren't selfish, we wouldn't have desires. Think carefully about this.

Since most people would rather evaporate into nothingness than be seen as selfish, they not only avoid expressing this quality, but they also go as far as to hide it from themselves. This is what causes us to censor ourselves within our minds, to ruminate and try with all our might to convince ourselves we aren't as bad as we believe deep down, in the dark recesses of our mind, where we believe we aren't worthy.

We have been conditioned to believe it's wrong to make ourselves the priority. We even tell each other that self-care isn't selfish to put ourselves at ease for attending to our needs and desires. But deep down we judge self-service in any form if we put it before the service of others. We feel a need to say something isn't selfish because we believe it is. This is why you hear the chanting often... "this isn't selfish, that isn't selfish." It's giving each other permission to be selfish while pretending it's not.

Since collectivism has become the way of life, readily accepted by the consensus despite discounting all the parts that make up that sum, you and I, the result has been a level of discontent all around. And, since the world won't change overnight to accommodate us, and the Missed Guidance less than likely to ever replace the misguidance, my encouragement is that you place your priority and concern with yourself and make the necessary changes you desire in your life.

So, while others continue along with the way things are going, you, the individual, can take charge of your life despite what others are doing. And, once others watch your life enhance, they will be inspired to step into their own shoes as well.

You may be thinking that this Missed Guidance is returning to Individualism versus Collectivism, and yes, in part it is, but it's taking a bigger, grander step for the self in the way I will present it to you.

I pray for the betterment of the world, and I contribute as much as I can without stepping over my own needs and desires. If you step on board and others do too, this will be a worthy step toward a Greater Good. Because it begins at your home with you.

The Missed Guidance, the Unreachable Dream, and the Essential Rules that follow are in support of you and your best life as long as you're willing to embody the important concept that you, as an individual, count as part of the whole, and that leaving yourself out any longer isn't an option. The guidance you have missed, the yearning you feel inside and a proactive path by which to improve your life by leaps and bounds, is available to you with your consent.

The willingness to take the Selfish Path and to do it with grace and intention is to free yourself while unburdening others to do the same, so that they can liberate their own lives too. You will learn within time that not only will you bring joy and peace into your own life, but your relationships with others will also thrive, and you will have a newfound love and respect for humanity.

So, before you partake in the Unreachable Dream and Essential Rules, and especially if you are feeling resistant, allow me to share with you the different expressions of selfishness that you will likely become if you continue to hide and deny this part of yourself, leave yourself out and resist change.

There are three variations of selfishness. The one that I encourage being, I refer to as Gracefully Selfish. The second is Greedily Selfish, and the third, Gravely Selfish. Their expressions are as follows:

GRACEFULLY SELFISH: Owning your rights to your basic human rights, your rights to attend to yourself, to live a happy life, to fulfill your dreams, and to consider yourself the most important person in your life, with the understanding and faith that by doing so you inspire others to do the same for themselves, and by shining your light you impact others to see theirs, and you spread your love all around without whining and fighting to get what you want because you are giving it to yourself.

GREEDILY SELFISH: Fed up with never getting what you want, over-exhausting yourself with everyone else's needs and desires. People pleasing your way through life in the hopes that someday it will all pay off and it will be your turn to reap. You are starting to see the light and have become resentful toward others for having to do what you no longer want to do for them. You whine about how no one appreciates you, reciprocates with you, and you slowly retreat into your own world. But you continue to do the same old, same old, despite how miserable you feel.

GRAVELY SELFISH: You're absolutely done with taking a back seat, and you see no other way than to take what ought to have been yours all along. Envy has reached dangerous heights and now you're doing things out of integrity and have become someone you never thought was possible. Even though deep down you thought you were bad and undeserving of good things, now you want justice for believing the BS. Lying and manipulating have become your normal way of communicating with others. You've reached the state of desperateness which will manifest itself in huge betrayals, e.g., cheating with your best friend's husband, backstabbing others at work, becoming abusive to others verbally (potentially physically), exploiting yourself and others, embezzling money, the results are endless. For further example, turn on *Dateline* or any true crime series to see what happens when people have had enough of never being or having enough.

It's been several years now since I made the choice to become Gracefully Selfish, and I can vouch for myself, as well as everyone that knows me, that I am a caring, loving and generous person. I give to charities regularly, honor and respect my family and friends, treat my clients with respect and professionalism and still take pride in my empathic nature.

But most of all, I am standing tall and proud of my newfound love and forgiveness for myself and the way I used to live, for I longed to be taken care of, to have others to depend on for my physical and emotional well-being, and thus burdened others to love and accept me.

Becoming Gracefully Selfish has changed my life in ways that make me dance like no one is watching, while inviting others to experience the love I have for myself, without burdening them to have to love me. It may be a desire, but it is no longer a need. As a result, I receive love letters and praise from friends, family, and clients alike, and feel honored and privileged to connect deeply with them in ways I never have as a People Pleaser.

It's fully up to you. Despite what everyone else is doing, you can change what *you're* doing.

I've been hesitant to broach this conversation in the past in fear of turning some people off, but I am no longer concerned with being liked. My greater agenda is to support others to like themselves. For if the world fills up with people who love themselves, what a worthy Greater Good that would be!

THE UNREACHABLE DREAM

I have a very close relationship with God.

I do not adhere to any espoused religion, even though I was raised Jewish and attended Hebrew and Sunday School as a child. I have remained proud of my Jewish heritage, both for cultural reasons and because my late parents were Holocaust survivors. I cannot imagine their experience and they barely spoke a word of it.

The reason I bring in God here is to share my strong belief that God loves us unconditionally. I haven't always felt this way, especially when I was younger and was struggling. But I believe this wholeheartedly today, and it is in knowing this, that I feel more joy and peace than ever before. And whenever I become afraid, I know I have misplaced my faith in fear and it's time to reconnect more deeply with God.

It's important for me to preface what I refer to as The Unreachable Dream, by making it clear that without feeling loved unconditionally by a source, we will struggle. I am not suggesting it's a must to become religious or spiritual, but without believing and having faith that there's something unseen and powerful that has your back, will make life appear arduous and heavy.

The Unreachable Dream, then, is our futile search for unconditional love with each other, our endless seeking to be loved without condition; hence, to be loved unconditionally, within our relationships with families, friends, partners, communities, ourselves and all of humanity. Not only do I insist it's improbable, but it is also impossible, unreachable and the biggest impediment that keeps us from connecting deeply with each other. It's a dealbreaker for obtaining healthy love and the glue that bonds us in toxic drama.

If it isn't bad enough to continue reaching for the unreachable, the expectation to be loved unconditionally is an excuse and set up to treat each other badly and get away with it, while filling our need to be loved for what we ourselves loathe. We burden each other to show us who we are so we don't have to go through the pain of doing the healing work ourselves.

Unfortunately, many if not all of us were wounded early in life. And, in our search to find closure and resolution to our pain, we latch on to others in hopes they will make us feel special, important, essential and loved; despite our flaws, idiosyncrasies, and the deep unworthiness we feel inside.

When we feel undeserving of a good life, plus lacking the permission to be selfish and reap, we must seek others to give us what we cannot take for ourselves. If you think about it carefully, being confident and loving toward oneself is seen as arrogant or being full of oneself. If we can't demonstrate love for ourselves and nurture ourselves in loving ways without being judged negatively, the only option is to seek out others to fill us up, love us, and deem us worthy. We burden each other to show us who we are, to hear us, to *get* us, and to make us feel essential and alive. And it makes perfect sense that we do this because innately we seek to survive. And the heart wants what the heart wants.

As humans, we are here to connect deeply, to love, and to find meaning and purpose in our lives. To be loved unconditionally sounds like nirvana, but if you carefully consider what it means to be loved without conditions, you will see more clearly the destructive nature of what this love implies. It would behoove us to let go of having such unrealistic expectations and stop seeking the Unreachable Dream. Let us instead seek mutual respect, admiration, consideration and love for one another and make sure we demonstrate this with our actions.

Setting boundaries and implementing consequences in our relationships is the only way to have connected, healthy unions. Relying on unconditional love to conquer all is naïve, and the expectation goes beyond the darkest expression of selfishness because it disregards others and places a burden on their shoulders.

There's a story I recently heard about a lovely, young couple, Avery and Paul, who are going through more than their fair share of challenges in life.

Avery is an avid People Pleaser who teaches her children to follow suit and serve the community with all they've got. She's presently facing major health issues after exhausting herself, while her young husband, Paul, is taking care of her, while picking up the slack to care for their two young children since she cannot. And while Avery is barely functioning, she makes time to take phone calls from people in the community who are struggling. While her husband fixes her dinner, instead of talking with him, she spends her time on the phone comforting others.

In their upstairs hallway, on a console, sits a weathered wooden sign that reads:

"Forever, For Always ... No Matter What."

Sounds beautiful, right? A commitment to love despite what happens, a love to last forever, for always. Isn't this what we all wish for? Isn't this why we keep at it, mustering through, trying harder, fighting with all our might to finally one day have that unconditional, no matter what, love?

Then there's a reality show hosted by a gorgeous married couple who support other couples to choose each other and live happily ever after. On one episode, the female host sitting beside her husband shares with the group that she knows with absolute certainty that *no matter what* happens, even if she were to fall victim to a car accident and lose her limbs, she knows her husband loves her with all his heart and would never leave her.

Amazing, right? That love we all yearn for. To be loved *no matter what*, without condition, without any outside circumstances threatening to break the bond. That unconditional love we seek in hopes that someday we can make a declaration boldly, assuredly as the female host who has unwavering faith that her love will stand the test of time.

Take a deep breath. I will be as tender as I can while bursting the *unconditional, no matter what bubble*. My predictions are not favorable.

Sadly, Avery and Paul will someday divorce. But even if they painstakingly decide to ride it out together, they will not be happy, and each will have personal regrets later in life. Their children will feel the effects of never ranking as special as their community who took away their parents' time and attention when they chose everyone else but them.

The gorgeous Barbie doll host who believes her Ken doll husband will never leave her will have a rude awakening when he has an affair and leaves her for a younger version. He was previously married to another stunning showstopper whom he emotionally abused on a different reality show, and they ended up going through a contentious divorce.

My harsh sarcasm is bold only to make my point even bolder. These people are lovely human beings, who deserve to be happy and live fully. They deserve respect, consideration, loyalty and commitment. But holding expectations of unconditional love and the *no matter what* happens agenda is playing with fire. It's just a matter of time before they get burned.

My strong encouragement is to drop the Unreachable Dream and instead treat each other with love, consideration and respect, while understanding that there is loss and consequences for bad behavior. No relationship can or should have to withstand the turmoil we put it through. No wonder everyone declares "Marriage is hard!"

I have been married more than once, and I loved being married. The hardship we endured was that we didn't like ourselves and burdened each other for validation. That was hard! We pointed our fingers at each other, and I chose to take on all the responsibility. I finally woke up and left.

Relationships are meant to thrive. If we rely on God for our source of unconditional love and learn to love ourselves deeply, we can treat each other with mutual respect and admiration. It's crucial that we be responsible for our own emotional well-being as we enter our relationships with others. It is no one's job to love us but our own.

And, no matter what, we should not expect to be loved no matter what.

Next!

THE ESSENTIAL RULES

The Essential Rules are my strategy for living in the present and living to the fullest. They are the Do's and Don'ts that support self-love and acceptance, while creating healthy relationships with others.

The Essential Rules pave the way for Red Flags to be seen with ease, curiosity, and the willingness to follow their direction because, once you become self-serving, you will live in protection of you.

I can't prove these Rules will take you to the life you desire, but if you're willing to give them your best effort, you will find the evidence you need to become a believer. You be the judge.

The Essential Rules support following your guidance and making the choices that serve YOUR best interests, which in turn will serve ALL OTHERS' interests. Once we are filled up with our own love and self-service, and embody the expression of Gracefully Selfish, what we most desire to do is to serve others. It truly is one of life's highest honors and joys.

The most loving person you can be for yourself and for others is to be **who you are**.

To connect with others in healthy ways, impact and inspire those we care about, and to serve the world in our unique way, we must nurture the relationship we have with ourselves *first*. This is the only chance we have if we want to live with joy and inner peace.

Imagine a world filled up with people who are filled up.

Now that's a Collective effect to be proud of.

FORGIVE YOURSELF FOR EVERYTHING.

Self-forgiveness is liberating and clears the path to the life that you seek. It delivers compassion and love, so that the Red Flags from the past can be processed. When you no longer beat yourself up or make yourself wrong for the choices you've made, you will see more clearly and objectively. With self-forgiveness you will come to understand that the choices you made at the time you made them made sense back then.

REFLECTION:

We yearn for our own forgiveness because, despite what others have done, we blame ourselves for what we could have or should have done and live with the shame of betraying ourselves.

To forgive yourself is a process that takes dedication and commitment. It is a daily practice that requires proactive effort, and it starts with the willingness to first make the choice.

If you are willing to forgive yourself, acknowledge this. It's the first step.

In my last book, *My Dearest Self, I Forgive You*, I include empowering statements of love and worth, reminders to own and claim your indispensable value, take a stand for yourself and honor who you are. This deepens the process of self-forgiveness.

The statement, "I forgive myself for *that*," works wonders when you remember past hurts. Instead of rehashing an experience or ruminating about it, use "*that*" as the reference for the experience. "I forgive myself for *that*" (whatever *that* experience was).

TREAT YOURSELF THE WAY YOU WOULD LIKE OTHERS TO TREAT YOU.

The relationship you have with yourself is the most important one. It will determine how deeply you know yourself, and it will affect the experiences you have with others. You are the judge, the model, the leader, the teacher. You will attract what you believe you deserve, and others will treat you according to the value you apply to yourself.

REFLECTION:

Look at how others treat you, and you will know how you feel about yourself.

You are frustrated because your partner doesn't hear you, listen to you, or care about what you think. It's obvious in their behavior toward you.

Your friends show up late to lunch even after you've voiced your disappointment time and again.

Examine these same scenarios in your relationship with you and you will find the mirror image:

How do you not listen to you, hear what you say, or care about what you think?

How do you show up for yourself in ways that are disappointing?

*Be gentle with yourself. It's not about beating yourself up, it's about changing the relationship you have with you and thus attracting the relationships you've always dreamed about.

**Master this Essential Rule and the world is your oyster.

DON'T RESIST OR CENSOR YOUR JUDGMENTS.

We have been taught and conditioned to believe it's not good to have judgments, especially the negative kind, so we resist and censor them, even within the safety of our mind.

REFLECTION:

The next time you have a conversation with someone, pay close attention to how you censor yourself and your feelings. You may apologize for tearing up or even make a statement and then judge the statement: "I feel really angry, although I know I shouldn't..." "I'm upset that you're late, but it's okay."

We find ourselves ruminating and even here, in the safety of our mind, we censor our thoughts and judgments, making ourselves bad or wrong. This is self-abusive, and it impacts choice-making in a very negative way. Without the freedom to have our judgments we cannot effectively make sense of our experiences or make accurate choices based on our perspective.

Do we want to censor our judgments with others? For sure! It would be hurtful to tell others what we're thinking all the time, especially if it's negative. But we must allow ourselves to think and feel what's there. It's human and it's normal.

Sometimes I have judgments that shock me, but I don't make myself wrong for having them. It's the way I bring compassion, love and acceptance to myself.

We must embrace both our darkness and our light.

FOLLOW YOUR GUT.

Are you familiar with how your gut speaks to you?

I can assure you that you are being informed. It's important you get clear with how messages are sent to you through your inner guidance. It may be a loud voice in your head, a strong thought, a physiological nudge or a feeling so profound you can't shake it. However your gut communicates with you, you can sense its message and detect the Red Flags that vie for your attention. It's in your best interest to listen and follow this guide. Your gut is right one hundred percent of the time.

REFLECTION:

Think back to a time when your gut was urging you to make a choice and you listened.

What happened?

Think of another time when you didn't listen.

What happened?

We are gifted with an inner knowing. Use it.

*Master this Essential Rule, it's a life saver and its directions are accurate.

STOP SECOND-GUESSING YOURSELF.

Stop doubting, rationalizing, justifying or second-guessing what you know. Stop hoping for others to convince you to go against what you resist and know to be true because you want an outcome so badly you will manipulate the circumstances to make it so.

REFLECTION:

As I mentioned in the section on Red Flags, when we receive information that goes against an outcome we desire, or when we have a large investment in a relationship, we will take a U-turn to avoid facing that which we fear. Don't create a worst-case scenario by second-guessing yourself. You know what you know. Lying to yourself won't change what's true and it won't stop a betrayal from happening. Much of our heartache is self-inflicted by not listening to ourselves.

It's time to embrace your power and appreciate that you have an inner guidance system that is accurate.

Trust it!

OWN YOUR PERSPECTIVE.

We each have a unique, personal experience of everything. We may see things differently than others do, and the meaning we give to the events of our lives may vary as well. It's important and essential that we honor the way we see things as *our* perspective and acknowledge its accuracy.

If we want to be flexible, have a meeting of the minds, and get along with others, we must allow them to have the same consideration. Don't dismiss your views to give into others, especially when it doesn't make sense to you. Agree to disagree. But it does pay to listen. You may learn something valuable.

REFLECTION:

Don't allow your insecurities to get the best of you and make others right and yourself wrong. Go with what makes sense to you.

Sometimes you will agree with others and sometimes you will want to scream. The political division in this country is a good example of this. We are likely to ignore each other because no one respects that we have different perspectives, and everyone believes they're right and others are wrong. I strongly suggest that all of us are right based on the way we see.

SAY NO AS OFTEN AS YOU FEEL IT.

NO is your power, your control, your right, your choice, your call, your worth.

Don't allow others to manipulate, coerce, convince or abuse your right to say **NO** to anything and everything you don't want to do.

REFLECTION:

Don't allow anyone to infer you don't have rights. Whether it's family or friends, make it clear.

We get intimidated by authority or people who abuse their power. Claim your right to say **NO**.

KNOW YOUR INTENTIONS WITH OTHERS.

Be clear about your relationships, what they mean to you and what your intentions are. Not all relationships are equal, and we look for certain experiences with specific people. It would behoove you to be clear about this, and it would also minimize a lot of heartache.

REFLECTION:
There is a difference between a best friend and a fair-weather friend. There are all sorts of relationships that range from meeting an acquaintance to finding a soulmate. It's important to know the relationships you desire and find yourself participating in. What do you hope to get out of these unions and what do you wish to put into them?

I use a Compartmentalizing System where I imagine positioning the people in my life. Sometimes they rank high and get promoted, and if they disappoint me, they get demoted. On occasion I give some of them their walking papers. I set my intentions according to their ranking.

If you want to live your best life, it pays to understand your relationships and your expectations of them along with the intentions you set for them. People will come and go. It's normal and it's healthy.

KNOW WHAT OTHERS WANT FROM YOU.

I always have a chuckle when someone declares "I'm being used!"

I can understand when someone is being taken advantage of, taken for a ride, or in a relationship that's built on bad intentions. But the greater truth is that we are using each other, 24/7. No one does something to gain nothing. Even people who claim to be selfless are using others to get a feeling or some sort of benefit. Don't fool yourself into thinking otherwise.

REFLECTION:

We get certain impressions by relating to others about what their interests with us may be, but aside from asking them, I encourage you to watch, listen, process and take your time. Remember to keep your antenna up for Red Flags, which is different than seeking them. We don't want to assume Red Flags are on the horizon unless we've already spotted one. But we do want to keep our blinders off, our ears open and our mind alert.

Once you know what someone wants from you, you can decide if this is a relationship you want to participate in or not.

TRUST FIRST IMPRESSIONS.

First impressions are interesting because they rely on an individual's perception and judgments when meeting others for the first time. With our personal expectations and limited information about others, it's interesting to watch how we choose to show up; what we say, what we wear, how we behave.

REFLECTION:

Think of a one-liner pick up at a bar: "Hey, honey, do you come here often?"

First impression: Uncreative, undemonstrative, insecure, doesn't value himself or you.

I'm not suggesting that our first impression encompasses all of who we are. Obviously not, but it is very telling, and it can be used to predict future behavior.

We are consistent in the ways we relate to others whether we do it effectively or not.

Think of relationships that have developed over time with someone you disliked at the very beginning, warmed up to, and discovered later that you were right about them when you first met? Pay attention and be careful who you invest your time and heart with.

DON'T BELIEVE WHAT CAN'T HAPPEN WON'T.

To avoid being blindsided, heeding the Red Flags is important. But even more so is the mindset that is prepared for the impossible to occur. Whatever you think you knew would never see the light of day already has. Did you really think Roe vs. Wade would be overturned?

In an ever-changing world, things can happen at an alarming pace, so be prepared to keep your eyes and ears open without believing you know the outcome.

REFLECTION:

It's important to protect yourself and your family. How you live, the way you think, the experiences you have are all crucial to your overall happiness.

But don't fall into a pattern where you naively skip along believing nothing bad can happen to you. Watch your back. Protect yourself. Be responsible for your safety.

HEAR THE WHISTLE BLOW, RED FLAGS ARE HERE.

It amazes me when people turn a deaf ear to a Whistleblower. Many of them have everything to lose and nothing to gain, except perhaps becoming a hero for sharing the illicit behavior of others they are privy to have information on. Do some have bad intentions? Perhaps. But most end up being discredited by corrupt entities and are ousted by the court of public opinion despite the evidence they have against evil doers. I believe Whistleblowers are the true advocates and heroes that live among us, and I salute them. They have undeniable courage, and they are here to wake us up.

REFLECTION:

It pays to know the full story and all the stories. These days Whistle Blowers are referred to as Conspiracy Theorists. Listen to them. Believe what makes sense to you but don't rob yourself of information that directly affects your life.

Don't kill the messenger.

DON'T SHARE THE RED FLAGS YOU SEE IN OTHERS WITH THEM.

This is challenging to do, but if you want accurate information, you wouldn't tell a conman that you're on to him. Many times, when we get information we'd rather not know, we'll hope to be convinced otherwise by sharing the information with the hope of getting an explanation that sends the Red Flags away.

REFLECTION:

It's becoming clear to me as I look back at past relationships where I was unhappy and continued to put forth effort despite how I felt, that even when I saw positive change I doubted it because of the Red

Flags I saw and my unwillingness to accept the relationship was toxic.

It's wise to become your own private investigator and not to disclose or discuss what you see with the suspect. Watch. Listen. Learn.

LOOK TO WHAT YOU HAVE NOT TO WHAT YOU'RE MISSING.

This rule will take you far if you commit to what it's asking of you. Despite many of us believing we are grateful, gratitude is an expression and a practice. It's easy to feel grateful when the electricity kicks back on after being out for days, and a different story to feel grateful for having electricity every day. We don't dwell on what we have, only on what we're missing.

REFLECTION:

The energy of *Gratitude* is within a high frequency, and it will attract that which also resides in a high frequency. The Law of Attraction, which never waivers, states that *like attracts like and opposites repel*. Aside from wanting to be happy and appreciative of your life, being grateful will attract the experiences that we often miss by hoping, wishing and wanting them.

Look at what you have and find gratitude for where you are, not where you want to go.

*Mastering this Essential Rule will bring magic into your life.

BE RADICALLY HONEST WITH YOURSELF.

It's time to put an end to the BS and stop lying about whatever you're lying to yourself about. Be radically honest with you. By radically, I mean completely, effortlessly, willingly. If you feel resistant, keep forgiving yourself for whatever ails you, whatever you hold against yourself in terms of grudges and resentments. Allow yourself to go forth telling yourself the painful, naked truth. Master this Rule and you will learn to trust yourself implicitly.

REFLECTION:

Nothing good comes from lying to ourselves, denying or disguising the truth, or trying to convince ourselves to be more patient and tolerant about whatever is making us miserable. To live your best life, you must trust the one person that is with you from the beginning to the end. **YOU!** Be radically honest with you and your life will change in ways you can't imagine now. You will also say goodbye to your therapist.

BE WILLING TO LOSE WHAT'S NOT IN YOUR BEST INTEREST.

Anyone who requires you to change who you are is not worthy of you. Never compromise yourself. Nothing is worth your worth. Nothing!

REFLECTION:

At times we can fall into the illusion that we need someone or something so much that we cannot survive otherwise. This is a lie. Don't fall for it.

Self-forgiveness is a soothing balm for the soul. Keep practicing the art of loving and forgiving you.

SET BOUNDARIES AND STICK TO THEM.

You set the bar when it comes to how you are treated by others. Boundaries are the notches on that bar.

REFLECTION:

A relationship without boundaries leaves you no leverage for a healthy, mutually respectful connection with anyone. In all relationships, we need to set boundaries. People know who they can disrespect and who they fear offending. Don't fall victim to other people's bad behavior because you fear setting boundaries.

HAVE DEALBREAKERS AND NEVER NEGOTIATE ON THEM.

It may hurt when others lie to us, but the greatest sting comes with lying to ourselves.

Hold your dealbreakers close and never negotiate with them.

REFLECTION:

There are certain things we do not tolerate, and whatever that is for you, you must honor and respect it as sacred; otherwise, forgiving yourself becomes an uphill battle. A betrayal is a betrayal, where a dealbreaker is a thousand betrayals, and letting one slide will feel as if you've sold your soul.

KNOW WHEN TO CUT TIES AND WALK AWAY.

As much as we want to connect with others and have long-lasting, loving relationships, it's important to know when to throw the towel in.

Abuse of any kind, disrespect and betrayals are unacceptable and it's important to know when it's time to distance yourself from all offenders.

REFLECTION:

I'm not sure why, as a society, we applaud staying together as if it were some kind of secret success despite the misery that many feel remaining complacent in toxic relationships.

I once asked a friend on his thirty-fifth wedding anniversary what his secret was.

His response, smiling widely: "No one in our family has ever divorced!"

My response: "That's not a secret; that's a life sentence."

To live your intended life, to be joyful and have inner peace, it's important to know your limits and when a relationship has run its course.

DON'T DEPEND ON THE ACCOLADES OF OTHERS TO FEEL BETTER.

We yearn most for our own love and acceptance. There is no standing ovation big enough than love and approval for the self.

REFLECTION:

NOW is a great time to bring forgiveness, love and compassion to yourself and to become aware of your worth, your greatness, and your invaluable uniqueness in this world. You are important, you matter, you count, and your presence here is vital.

It is your job to love yourself. It's no one's purpose to do this for you.

DON'T GIVE ULTIMATUMS OR SETTLE FOR THEM.

Having to convince anyone of your worth comes from a wounded place of not feeling deserving or good enough. Confidence comes from walking away, not toward others that don't believe in you.

Your worth is not negotiable.

REFLECTION:

Feeling the need to give an ultimatum is a big Red Flag. My biggest regrets are having married more than once with an ultimatum on the table. It's important to be objective and protective when deciding with people who cannot.

LISTEN TO THE RED FLAGS OTHERS SHARE WITH YOU.

Whereas we ultimately want to make our own choices, it pays to listen to others that care about us and the Red Flags they see that we may miss.

REFLECTION:

It never hurts to hear what others have to say. You don't have to take anyone's advice about anything. If you are secure in your perspective and confident in your choices, the more objective you are, the more likely you will make decisions that support your best interest. Listening to others doesn't hurt.

DON'T BE BULLIED INTO FORGIVING ANYONE FOR ANYTHING.

Forgiveness of others doesn't work for everyone. In my case it made me a better People Pleaser and had me re-enter relationships that I left. You don't need to forgive anyone to let go of pain and heartache. In fact, some people find it easier to let go of a grudge by giving themselves permission NOT to forgive.

REFLECTION:

Do what works for you, and don't allow others to tell you what's best for you. I love the process of Self-forgiveness because it gives us full control, and we cannot depend on the forgiveness of others. For some people it feels self-loving to withhold forgiveness.

DON'T MAKE EXCUSES FOR YOUR OFFENDERS.

Stop using people's horrific childhoods to explain away their bad behavior. Not only is it diminishing their character and disempowering to their potential, it enables them to remain a victim and to keep offending you.

REFLECTION:

Deep down I believe we all crave discipline and don't get off on being let off the hook. Also, many people use this excuse to deflect responsibility. It's time to hold everyone accountable.

FORGIVE OFFENDERS DISCREETLY AND DON'T LET THEM KNOW.

If you choose to forgive the people who have offended and betrayed you, do so with discretion.

REFLECTION:

If it helps you to forgive others for their transgressions, despite not forgetting or condoning anything they've done, do so for you. Telling someone that you have forgiven them, unless it's your intention they must know, may feel regretful later. People who display their bad behavior and are granted forgiveness from others tend to repeat their offenses because they seem to get away with them and gain other's forgiveness to boot. Personally, I think there's some warranted justice in keeping them in the dark and letting them wonder.

BE YOUR GREATEST CONFIDANTE.

Consult yourself for information and answers. If you consider the questions we ask others, we're likely wanting to be convinced about a choice we're about to make that we question making. Wouldn't it be nice to take our own advice, knowing that no one knows what's best for us than us?

REFLECTION:

Have a conversation with yourself. Imagine that you are giving advice to a good friend you care about. You have everything you need to make the best choices for you. Be your greatest source of information and follow your heart.

DON'T BREAK PROMISES YOU MAKE TO YOURSELF.

This rule is so important in terms of living a full, happy life. Self-love requires your commitment and keeping your word. If it's not enough that others disappoint us, not showing up for ourselves with consistency and commitment is a big kick in the butt. It has us lose trust in the only person whose love and acceptance are paramount: Ourselves.

REFLECTION:

Be cognizant of the promises you make to yourself and make them the priority. You are the only person that can declare and claim your worth. You must prove to yourself what you try so hard to prove to others.

BE VULNERABLE WITH YOUR THERAPIST/COACH.

Sorry, Brene, but I must disagree.

Yes, it's true that everyone professes to want to be loved unconditionally; to be heard, understood, and seen. But the moment we unleash our vulnerabilities we risk killing the passion and instilling fear into each other which often creates guardedness, suspicion and harsh judgements.

In addition, sharing deeply is used against us, especially when the relationship ends. Watch some of the reality shows on relationships, and you can watch things fall apart in real time.

I am not suggesting we don't have deep, connected relationships. We are here to love. And I do believe it's important to share deeply, but when it comes to spilling our guts, leave that for sessions with a professional.

REFLECTION:

Being a Life Coach for fourteen years and doing extensive healing work on myself both in therapy and coaching, whenever I considered a friend or partner my therapist or became theirs, it was a nightmare, and it didn't bode well. I was even married to a mental health provider that played mind games and used my vulnerabilities against me. I was traumatized.

We face big challenges in childhood and in life, and seeking counsel from professionals is the best answer. It's our responsibility to enter relationships emotionally healthy and to maintain our wellness throughout our lives. Let's stop burdening each other and love each other instead.

ALLOW YOUR MEMORIES TO REMAIN IN REAL TIME.

It makes me sad that so many people, including myself at times in my past, have diminished good memories when a betrayal happens later. The story shouldn't end because it ended badly. Allow memories to remain as they happened in real time even when you tuck them away.

REFLECTION:

Even when a betrayal is so big we want to erase the entire relationship from our mind, the memories still exist within our psyche. To diminish them is an injustice to ourselves and what we did for love.

I hear this phrase often as a Coach who supports others in healing: *None of it seems real now.*

I can vouch for the pain of betrayals, making everything appear as if it all was a lie, and in some cases it can be. But either way, our experience at the time was real and the memory should be honored as real at the time, even when we choose not to remember.

Remember Brian? The boyfriend that conned me into a Ponzi scheme? Despite his intentions and how our relationship ended, the good times we had were real. They are real memories. I may not choose to cherish them, but it pays to keep them intact.

BECOME THE PARENT TO YOURSELF YOU WISH YOU HAD AS A CHILD.

This Rule isn't designed to criticize our parents or to take away any gratitude we have for the life they gave us and for all they did do for us. Instead, it's a practice that supports moving on from childhood neglect and trauma, with treating ourselves in loving, compassionate, nurturing ways from now on.

REFLECTION:

As an adult, it's imperative we treat ourselves well and nurture ourselves like we would an innocent, loving child. We must become parents to ourselves and be the kind of nurturing support we always hoped for. This is a profoundly essential practice, and it will support you in learning to love and trust yourself implicitly.

*Master this rule and you will feel deeply supported.

LEAVE LOST TRUST UNFOUND.

Once trust is lost in a relationship, allow it to remain lost. You can stay wherever you desire but be honest with yourself while you do. Broken trust is broken trust. I liken it to gluing together a broken vase. Tread lightly.

REFLECTION:

This is a Dealbreaker for me. Once I lose trust for someone it's over.

Think long and hard about what trust means to you.

Choose how you want to live and those you want to surround yourself with.

I have people in my life whom I do not trust, and I can have a pleasant relationship with them. But when it comes to my heart or anything else I hold dear, I do not share with them.

NEVER LOSE YOUR CURIOSITY AND INVESTIGATE EVERYTHING.

Curiosity may have killed the cat, but the damage that ensues for those who remain ignorant is in a different league altogether.

REFLECTION:

Don't live your life being clueless or waiting for things to change.

DON'T THINK THEY WON'T DO TO YOU WHAT THEY DID TO THEM.

Don't assume that people who treat others badly will not repeat the same behavior in their relationship with you. It's not only likely, but also predictable.

It pays to let others talk.

Listen. Sooner or later, everyone reveals who they are.

REFLECTION:

Keep your eyes open, prick your ears, and watch your back.

DON'T BELIEVE EVERYTHING YOU HEAR.

Whether we like it or not, we all lie. Yes. All of us. Even you. The Red Flags come bearing big lies. Mind them.

REFLECTION:

If you're one of those people who believes you don't lie, allow me to support you in taking responsibility.

If you cannot think of a time when you have lied, believe you never have or will, or better yet, believe you are completely honest, answer the following questions:

1. Have you told your friend she looks great when your honest judgment is that she looks awful, tired and old?
2. Have you lied to yourself about someone or something to make yourself feel better?
3. Have you amped up your resume because you wanted a job so badly you didn't think it could hurt to exaggerate a little?
4. What about your age? Have you lied about that?

Breathe. We all lie. It's normal.

But when it comes to the big, deceptive lies, the betrayals, and the intent to hurt and harm, those are the lies we must pay attention to. Red Flags come in handy when it comes to big lies because, unlike white lies, most people try to hide their deception. Pay attention when things appear *off*.

A good practice is to accept fifty percent of everything you hear as the possible truth and throw the other fifty percent away. It takes time to get to know someone. Take the time.

COMMON RED FLAGS: HEED THEM.

- Inconsistencies in stories.
- Avoiding eye contact.
- A roving eye.
- An inability to read a room accurately.
- Fast and furious when getting to know you.
- Making excuses and deflecting bad behavior.
- Questions that are met with defensiveness.
- A need to control everyone and everything.
- Accusations that are completely unwarranted.
- Gaslighting.
- Constant complaining.
- Possessiveness.
- Never admitting fault.

- Not taking responsibility for anything.
- Overly flexible – Having no preferences.
- Overly complimentary
- Having no friends.
- History of bad relationships.
- Commitment phobia.
- Blaming and shaming everyone.
- Not wanting solutions to problems.
- Overly needing attention.
- Unwilling to negotiate.

DON'T SHARE WITH OTHERS WHAT YOU DON'T WANT SHARED.

Despite asking others for their loyalty and respect not to divulge things you share with them, you cannot count on them to keep their mouth shut. Don't trust anyone with information that is sacred and question yourself for having the need to share it in the first place.

REFLECTION:

I once heard that our need to share sensitive information has more to do with our desire to release whatever weight it is we are carrying; that we secretly want our secrets out. So, think carefully about this choice. Because the moment you tell someone, you risk everyone finds out.

DON'T COMMENT ON SOCIAL MEDIA POSTS YOU DISAGREE WITH.

Posting on social media is like getting a tattoo. Even though you can remove body art you no longer relate to, what you post on social media remains. Choose your words carefully.

REFLECTION:

Social media can be great to connect with others, build your business, and even meet new people. But it has a dark side too. Be careful what you post and comment on.

ONE WARNING IS ENOUGH. TRUST IT.

There's no need to wait for the other shoe to drop when many others are lying on the floor.

REFLECTION:

Turning away from guidance won't stop the wakeup calls from getting louder.

Take your warnings seriously and heed them.

TRUST IN YOUR JOURNEY.

We each have a unique journey that is solely ours. Mind your journey. Be grateful for your experiences. Live your intended life.

REFLECTION:

Don't waste your time getting into other people's business. Stop trying to figure others out, fix them, change them or manipulate the circumstances.

Your journey represents your life. Focus on you. Remember: the way we treat ourselves we will be treated. Whenever we falter from this Rule, things go downhill quickly.

Nurture the relationship you have with yourself. Hold it sacred.

TURN YOUR KINDNESS AND COMPASSION SKILLS ON YOU.

It's time to give yourself the time and attention you deserve and to shower yourself with love.

REFLECTION:

Take the time, love, attention, compassion, sympathy, empathy, and care that you extend to others and amp it up on you.

We most yearn for our own love and approval.

CHANGE WHAT ISN'T WORKING FOR YOU.

Stop doing the same old, same old when you aren't seeing the results you want.

REFLECTION:

Change happens regardless of the choices we make.

Even though we cannot know the outcome of everything, we certainly can impact that outcome by the choices we make.

Make different choices.

DON'T BE A SLAVE TO YOUR ELECTRONIC DEVICES.

There's nothing more distracting to living life than our electronic devices that we have become addicted to.

REFLECTION:

Much of our stress and exhaustion comes from our inability to cut ourselves off from whatever or whoever needs us in the moment.

I have made it a practice to no longer be a slave to my phone or any other device or person that demands attention.

If you want to live a peaceful, joyful life, it pays to stop missing out on your life and allow yourself to miss the calls and emails instead.

DON'T WASTE YOUR TIME WITH PEOPLE WHO WASTE YOUR TIME.

There's nothing more annoying to me than people who take calls when they are dining with you. It's not only rude to you, but it's a big Red Flag that reveals how they value you and themselves.

REFLECTION:

I once heard a story told by one of my favorite teachers and mentors, the great, Carolyn Myss. Not only is she a famous medical intuitive, author, and sought after speaker, I could only dream of the opportunity to have a private dinner with her. It would be like winning the lottery.

She shared a story with a group of us about a dinner engagement she had with a friend.

"When I arrived at the restaurant, my friend was on her cell phone. She barely acknowledged me and did not try to hang up, instead, she continued to speak on the phone, engage and laugh for a few minutes. She must have thought when I stood up and walked away that I went to the Ladies Room, but I left the restaurant and went home."

BOLD MOVE, CAROLYN!

If you're expecting an important call that trumps the dinner you have scheduled with a friend, it may behoove you to stay at home with your phone and take all the calls you want.

We make choices.

DON'T BE AFRAID TO LET PEOPLE KNOW HOW YOU REALLY FEEL.

Many people chant these days about watching your reactive behavior. While I feel it's good practice to always be respectful, there are situations where it pays to react and let someone know your position.

REFLECTION:

We are teachers for each other and anyone at the receiving end of a reaction has an opportunity to learn something.

BE SELECTIVE
WHEN CHOOSING FRIENDS.

I've heard it said that if we can count our friends on one hand, we're lucky.

REFLECTION:

A few meaningful relationships are a blessing.

Be good and true to yourself and you will attract relationships that fill you with joy.

Choose wisely with your heart.

MAKE SURE YOUR CHOICES ARE YOUR CHOICES.

A choice that originates from your heart will feel different than a "should" choice or a choice someone else prefers you make.

REFLECTION:

Your gut plays a big part when it comes to choosing from your heart. It will alert you to the Red Flags that indicate the choice you're about to make may not be yours.

This Rule is so important for living your intended life.

*Master this Rule and you will remain true to yourself.

DON'T EXPECT OTHER PEOPLE TO STICK UP FOR YOU.

It's important to not rely on others to have your back or defend you. That is your job, and no one gets the point across better than you.

REFLECTION:

I used to get upset when others didn't take my side, agree with me, or stick up for me when someone offended me. What I didn't realize at the time was that I didn't have my back and depended on others to protect me. Reference Rule #2: Others will treat us the way we treat ourselves. If we aren't defending ourselves no one will stand up to defend us either.

MAKE YOUR VOICE COUNT.

If you don't speak up, it will feel as if your voice doesn't count. The ball is in your court.

REFLECTION:

It's important to participate in discussions and to start them too, otherwise it will feel as if you are left out or don't belong. It's up to us to participate.

ALLOW YOURSELF TO HEAR NEGATIVE FEEDBACK.

Not everyone will agree with us and listening to negative feedback only stings when we don't have our back.

REFLECTION:

I get excited when someone gives me negative feedback or disagrees with me and I have a completely neutral feeling about it. It's evidence to me that I am standing stronger and taller in who I am and how I feel.

For someone in her past who allowed others to define her, I can say with conviction that this is no longer a part of my repertoire.

DON'T OFFER FAVORS YOU DON'T WANT TO DO.

People throw phrases around so lightly and often. It's phony. Don't say it if you don't mean it.

REFLECTION:

It's not fair to offer gestures to others when you don't mean them.

"Call me if you need anything" is a typical phrase people throw around because most people don't take them up on it. Think carefully and only offer what you are willing to do.

THINK CAREFULLY BEFORE MAKING AMENDS.

Sometimes the best choice is to let sleeping dogs lie.

REFLECTION:

Many people don't realize that making amends isn't always a good choice. There's the potential that our act of grace may rehash a memory for another and cause a wound to reopen. We can apologize to others in the safety of our mind by visualizing making amends with them.

I believe that we can deliver communication telepathically and energetically and others will feel it. And once we forgive ourselves for the offenses we afflict on others, we can move powerfully forward without having to depend on their forgiveness, which is not a guarantee.

DON'T LEAD PEOPLE ON.

Don't spend time with people you don't enjoy being with until something better comes along. It's not only disrespectful to them, but it also prevents new people from coming into your life.

REFLECTION:

It's easy to fall into routines and patterns, even with the people we surround ourselves with. But it's better to be alone for a while and do some soul searching than staying put and going through the motions for fear of being alone.

MAKE TIME TO BE ALONE AND BOND WITH YOU.

If you truly want to get to know who you are, it's imperative that you spend time by yourself, with yourself, bonding.

REFLECTION:

Learning to love your own company, while losing your fear of being alone, will take you very far in life.

Bonding with you is essential. Consider this time sacred.

MAKE LOTS OF ROOM FOR LOVE.

There are many kinds of relationships and all types of love. Make room for as much love as you can muster. It's essential to love.

REFLECTION:

I used to believe I needed a romantic relationship to love. I learned my lesson the hard way. There are so many ways to love, and romance isn't at the top of my list anymore. I revel in my love for my fur babies, my friends, and people I deeply resonate with on a spiritual level.

SURROUND YOURSELF WITH BEAUTY.

Another essential ingredient in a full life is to appreciate the surroundings we spend our time in.

REFLECTION:

Make your surroundings pleasing to you. It has a tremendous effect on your mood.

When I find myself in a room that's aesthetically beautiful or decorated in a way that pleases me, I am happy.

OWN YOUR ANGER.

Our anger is directly related to our power and our purpose. Don't minimize your feelings.

REFLECTION:

Anger is an important human emotion and it's our birthright to feel it.

Like any emotion, anger needs to be felt, processed and expressed.

The more you allow yourself to have your feelings, the more control you have over how you express them.

Breathe.

BOW OUT OF COMMITMENTS YOU QUESTION.

Give yourself permission to get out of something that no longer feels right to you.

REFLECTION:

Keeping a commitment just because you made the commitment isn't a good enough reason to stick it out.

It's admirable to hold our integrity to high standards, but sometimes there are extenuating circumstances that get in the way. When Red Flags guide you to move in another direction, excuse yourself and bow out.

DON'T BLAME YOURSELF FOR NOT KNOWING.

We don't have ESP, and we can't always predict what others will do. Red Flags come in handy, but even with their guidance we have no control over other people's behavior.

REFLECTION:

Don't make yourself wrong when something happens that you didn't suspect.

It's time to amp up self-compassion and comfort yourself.

PROTECT WHAT YOU LOVE.

There's nothing wrong with being protective and guarded, especially as it concerns you and anyone or anything you love.

REFLECTION:

It pays to be mindful and not to get into anything with anyone where you have everything to lose and they have nothing to lose. Some people just like to cause trouble.

COUNT YOUR BLESSINGS TWICE.

It's one thing to feel blessed and another to practice gratitude for what you have and all that you are.

REFLECTION:

Sometimes it's helpful for me to think of scenarios where I no longer have what's dear to me in my life presently. It snaps me into a grateful mood instantly.

DON'T COMFORT THE PEOPLE WHO HURT YOU WHEN THEY'RE SORRY.

Comforting the people who have disappointed us, which is notorious for People Pleasers, is not only inappropriate and exhausting but also self-abusive. Don't do it.

REFLECTION:

When others disappoint you, don't jump to make them feel better about it. Your feelings matter more.

BE SELECTIVE WITH WHAT YOU HOPE FOR.

It pays to be realistic when it comes to where you place hope and how long you keep hoping.

REFLECTION:

It's nice to aim high, but many ideals are unreachable. I'm not suggesting you settle for anything, but don't keep hoping against hope for something that's hopeless.

*Master this Rule and your disappointments will become far and few.

ACCEPT THAT YOU HAVE CHANGED.

It can be frustrating when we grow while others remain the same.

REFLECTION:

Breaking the status quo does not ensure everyone is on board.

Accept that you are on a different playing field when you make changes and grow, and others may resent the change.

Sometimes this can end a relationship or cause some drama.

Be where you are, process your feelings, and find compassion for others' fear of loss. But never give up on you.

DON'T GIVE OTHERS CREDIT FOR YOUR GROWTH.

Whereas our teachers support us in learning, we must do the work. Give credit where credit is due and don't underestimate your efforts.

REFLECTION:

Some people have the arrogance to believe you cannot grow, survive or thrive without them.

NONSENSE!

No one is responsible for your potential or for your greatness. They may deserve a thank you, but never a medal.

BE PROUD!

DON'T CONFRONT THEM, WITHHOLD INSTEAD.

Sometimes, no words speak the loudest.

REFLECTION:

Confronting others isn't always the best option, while saying nothing stings more.

When I'm disappointed with someone that I'd rather not confront, I withhold instead. It not only gets the message across beautifully, but it also has others wondering where you stand.

Nothing like a good mystery.

*Master this Rule and people will know they cannot mess with you.

DANCE LIKE NO ONE IS WATCHING.

We are in control of our mindset and our mood. It is possible to be happy despite what's going on.

REFLECTION:

Sooner or later, when you keep dancing like no one is watching, you will attract a crowd.

People want to be around the people they most want to be like.

Be an inspiration.

DON'T MAKE YOURSELF AVAILABLE FOR THOSE WHO DON'T CARE.

When your efforts go unappreciated or unnoticed, stop making yourself available.

REFLECTION:

At times we may be desperate, but we're not stupid. It's obvious when people don't care as much as we do, or when our efforts are ignored.

Don't step over yourself to please anyone, especially when it doesn't matter to them.

TUNE OUT THE NAYSAYERS.

Have you seriously considered the people whose judgments you took to heart, and the thoughts you took to bed at night wondering and worrying if you'd ever be enough?

REFLECTION:

Have you considered the lack of qualifications these judges had to define you?

When I think of the people I looked up to and admired, whose opinions mattered, whose judgments were set in stone, I must have a big laugh about it because many of them were certified losers.

This declaration is not about anger or resentment but instead a byproduct of wisdom and growth.

KNOW WHEN THEIR YES IS REALLY A NO.

Use your noodles and read the energy. It's useful to know when people are lying or kissing up to you. Don't accept a yes that you know is a no.

REFLECTION:

It pays to study body language and to know the people we spend time with. Remember, everyone lies or says things they don't mean. Connect the dots and know the deeper story.

TELL THE PEOPLE YOU LOVE THAT YOU LOVE THEM.

Salute the love you see in others and make sure you let them know you love them.

REFLECTION:

I don't throw the phrase *I love you* around like many others do. When I feel it and mean it, I say it.

Show your love.

PRACTICE LOVING GESTURES WITH YOURSELF.

You will be amazed at the magic that unfolds once you start loving up on yourself.

REFLECTION:

Blowing kisses at yourself in the mirror, kissing the tops and palms of your hands, wrapping your arms around your body, tenderly applying lotion on your legs and feet, hugging your pillow, saying thank you for you, telling yourself: *I love you.*

There are limitless opportunities to demonstrate your love for yourself even and especially if you don't feel it.

Fake it till you feel it is a practice that will have you become a master at manifesting all good things. Love begets love.

*Master this Rule and you will Rule the world.

OWN YOUR GREATNESS AND SHINE.

Even when others don't see the greatness in you, you must see it and shine.

REFLECTION:

When I get the feeling that others aren't impressed with me or seem indifferent, I say this phrase to myself: "They don't know who I am." It immediately shifts me into appreciating myself and holding pride in who I am, despite their nonchalant attitude. This helps to shift from the *not good enough* wound to I'm *super special*.

It may sound arrogant to you, and I am going to suggest that if you don't like arrogance, you don't appreciate confidence either because arrogance is a bold expression of the latter.

Own your greatness.

WHEN YOU SENSE DISINTEREST IN WHAT YOU'RE SAYING, STOP TALKING.

Don't waste your time, energy, breath, knowledge and effort on people whose eyes are glazing over.

REFLECTION:

Speak where you are heard and you will no longer feel unheard.

Your voice counts in all the right rooms.

WHEN YOUR KINDNESS ISN'T APPRECIATED, DON'T BECOME KINDER.

Don't amp up your people-pleasing skills when it's clear your effort isn't desired. Not everyone likes being doted on and some have a hard time receiving kindness. Sometimes it's kinder to tone it down.

REFLECTION:

Some people get anxiety around having to reciprocate the kindness of others.

Learning how to read a room and sense people's energy will go a long way.

Take a *no thank you* as an affirmative no and leave things alone.

DON'T WASTE YOUR TIME WITH PEOPLE WHO WASTE THEIRS.

People who waste their own time aren't pleasant to be around, so don't waste your time with them.

REFLECTION:

Value and worth are fun to be around.

Mind your energy.

PRACTICE QUIETING YOUR MIND.

It's healthy to incorporate practices that quiet your mind and bring you peace. Whether you choose to meditate or listen to relaxing music, you must quiet your mind.

REFLECTION:

Give your busy mind a rest.

*Master this Rule and you will experience better moods.

MAKE FUN AND LEISURE A PRIORITY.

No matter how busy you are, it's essential you make time to have fun, to play, to leisurely spend time doing nothing or something that you find relaxing.

REFLECTION:

Take something off your plate or say no to a previous commitment. Fun and leisure are essential for a balanced life.

*Master this Rule and you will get more things accomplished and do them more efficiently.

TALK TO YOURSELF WITH COMPASSION.

The way we speak to ourselves is so important. Watch what you say, how you say it, and don't under any circumstances call yourself hurtful names.

REFLECTION:

Calling yourself stupid or any other hurtful name, even if you think you're joking, isn't received well by your psyche. Be loving, compassionate and gentle with your communication with you.

*Master this Rule and you will soften hearing your own voice.

PRAY FOR ALL THOSE SUFFERING AND DONATE TO CHARITIES.

Sometimes we can feel helpless when others suffer, especially when we have no control over their circumstances. Prayer is powerful and it travels to all corners of the world.

Giving to charities is such a sacred honor and privilege. It is something we must practice.

REFLECTION:

Even though we cannot change things, we can impact change, and we can certainly support others that cry out for help.

*Master this Rule and you will fill up with joy.

BECOME YOUR SACRED ADMIRER.

Watch the magic unfold as you become kinder and more loving with you.

REFLECTION:

A **Sacred Admirer** is not only in awe of themselves but who considers their existence invaluable to the world. They understand that their purpose is specific and one that speaks to their heart while bestowing upon others the precious gifts only they can offer. A **Sacred Admirer** considers that if they were gone, their loss would be missed and mourned, not because they people-pleased or bribed others to like and approve of them, not because they sacrificed themselves and their families to show up for strangers, not because they contributed to the community, but instead, because their love, gratitude and respect for themselves was so admired, envied and desired by all.

The undying belief in ourselves and our worth is what we all yearn for, and it allows us to authentically reach out to others and the world in loving ways. A **Sacred Admirer** knows their value and they never question their worth.

THE AFTER PARTY

The After Party is an invitation to free yourself from the emotional burdens of the past, to celebrate the present and to move steadfastly toward the future with faith that your life is on track.

If you are willing to allow the Red Flags to guide you from this day forward, to incorporate the Essential Rules into your daily life, to make yourself your priority, and to commit to your happiness, you will embark on the path to your intended life.

Each of us has experienced heartache in some form or another, and it's time to clear away the obstacles that keep us from living our best lives, that hold us back from our goals, and that influence us to give up on our dreams. Blame and shame, grudges and resentments, outdated beliefs and unrealistic expectations are the dark energy that keeps our joy at bay. It's time to clean our inner house.

If you're like me, you believe in karma and justice, in *what goes around comes around*. But for many, the victory of witnessing offenders held accountable for their transgressions won't likely see the light of day, and even if they do, it doesn't happen in a way that appeases us. Don't fret because this doesn't mean offenders won't get what's coming to them.

It's important to remember that karma knows every address, and if we choose to trust this and not be attached to how justice is delivered, we can rest assured it will come at the right time with the right lesson.

If you've made it this far in the book, I think it's obvious my intention is to support you in moving toward the life you desire and to take charge of your choices. To do this, it's essential that you be radically honest when cleaning your inner house to make sure there is no residual gunk left behind.

Despite people touting forgiveness, and how cathartic an experience it is, I believe that many people feel incomplete because their offenders seem to get away with their bad behavior while they continue to struggle and stay stuck. I also feel that, if given the option, most people would fess up that a little justice wouldn't hurt and some harmless revenge would feel damn good.

I am going to suggest and encourage that you trust in karma to do its job because what goes around does come around, and all of us will complete the circle at some time or another. Yes. All of us. Including you.

I remember a time in my life when a love interest dismissed me in a very offensive way. I recall declaring how I would never treat someone in such a bad way and then realized I did exactly that same thing to someone years before.

Whether we know it or not or like it or not, we do get what's coming to us. It is to learn, and it is essential so that we know ourselves deeply and take responsibility for our behavior. We hurt people too.

Some of my spiritual cronies would say I'm in an "ego" conversation when it comes to forgiveness, but since I've been on both sides, the *let's let go and love everyone, forgive, forgive, forgive*, and the *ego's desire for payback*, I can say from personal experience that a little of both is the perfect balance.

If you leave the dark thoughts to fester, they grow and block you in all areas of life. A friendship between ego and heart makes for a healthy adventure here on earth. Your ego may play mind games but hating it or pushing it away will only give it leverage over you. As the adage goes, *keep your enemies close.*

It's normal to want revenge and it's human to want justice. But we must be careful how we internalize our anger because we don't want to lose our livelihood to get back at someone. Violence is never acceptable, and holding onto resentment will not move us forward. As the proverb goes: "Holding onto anger is like drinking poison expecting the other person to die."

Also, it's pertinent to know wishing someone ill may come back on you. You must be careful what you wish for because your requests are more powerful than you suspect. A happy mindset isn't inundated with hate. If we trust and have faith that no one is spared their lessons, we can relax into the knowing that The Universe is taking care of our wishes.

To make a bold point, I have my own theory on the injustice that shocked the world when O.J. Simpson was acquitted for the June 12, 1994 murders of his ex-wife, Nicole Brown Simpson and her friend, Ronald Goldman.

Without including the details of the media circus trial and all the unkosher goings-on's, (there's a wealth of information on google if you want to familiarize yourself with how it played out), the verdict left people reeling in disbelief that such an injustice can happen. But it does and it did.

Since karma is based on cause and effect, I thought about the events that transpired during and after the trial and up until the death of O.J. Simpson on April 10, 2024, to put together a karmic effect that would trump a death penalty or life sentence. And I found one that puts me at peace.

O.J. Simpson was proclaimed a hero by many. And if you're familiar with the narcissistic personality, he lived and breathed attention and praise. Evidence presented at trial wreaked of his guilt and, despite O.J.'s lawyers' spinning tales of his innocence, his acquittal did not give him back his life. He may have been a free man in our eyes, but he was hardly free. He was rejected and abandoned by his cronies and shamed by many of his fans.

Had O.J. been sentenced to life in prison, he, in my strong opinion, could have and likely would have become a hero for a different cause, and a worthy one the world could use if he chose to admit his guilt and become the voice for domestic violence. His celebrity would have had an impact even from inside prison walls on the serious nature of domestic violence and its fatal effects on everyone involved. He would have maintained a huge fan base and an overflowing ego cup.

A narcissist can thrive anywhere if they are the center of attention. But instead, he was seen as a monster and a nobody, his greatest fear, for deep down I believe he loathed himself. You can't commit this kind of crime when you are emotionally healthy and love yourself.

His life remained in shambles and continued its demise until his death from cancer in 2024. It may not have been the justice his victims would have bestowed; but nonetheless, it was a nightmare for him.

I've heard about cold cases that have reopened, where a suspect is caught and punished thirty years later. Some call it justice a little too late. But what if their capture happened at a time in their life where they were thriving; a time when they ended someone else's young and happy life? My theory being that we get what we deserve when the impact is personally the most devastating to the individual.

Hopefully, the heartache you've experienced is not of the criminal kind, but nevertheless, I believe we like to see others held accountable for hurting us in some way. Getting away scot-free just feels unfair. And we must accept the consequences of our offenses too.

So, getting back to trusting the Karma Gods and having faith that justice is imminent, we can let go of the desire for personal revenge because this will never serve us. But that doesn't mean we can't express and channel our anger in ways that leave us feeling empowered. We may not get to hold our offenders accountable in a way we would have liked, but not getting the justice we want doesn't mean we don't get to be justified for having a personal claim in seeing others take responsibility for their actions.

I have created a F**k You Declaration that I hope will suffice. It works like a charm for me. It's a way to stick it to the people who have hurt us by growing, evolving, and saying our peace without having to have any contact with them.

And first, I provide instructions to take a Justice Journey down Red Flags Lane to bring about some clarity for the experiences you wish to tuck away, the people you choose to have justice with, and the opportunity to withhold forgiveness if you wish.

As I've mentioned before, for some, me included, forgiveness isn't always the best option. It made me a better People Pleaser, holding more resentment toward myself and overly taking responsibility for everyone and everything. It was exhausting, frustrating, and wreaking havoc in my life.

Self-forgiveness gives you full control over the part you played in all your experiences, the blame and shame you hold against yourself, and it delivers an acceptance and inner peace that forgiving others pales in comparison. And it made me kinder and more generous with others.

So, don't let anyone bully you into having to forgive anyone unless it is your desire to do so. It's one hundred percent possible to let go without forgiving anyone, but you must forgive yourself. I am a believer that everyone deserves God's forgiveness, but that not everyone deserves *my* forgiveness. This makes me feel powerful and justified.

The good news is that once you give yourself the freedom to feel whatever you're feeling and to address your offenders in a safe, healthy way, in time you may soften and become more objective to the experience once you are no longer emotionally invested, and you arrive at a place of acceptance and peace reaping the growth and gifts this experience has brought you and how your life today is better for having survived it.

TAKING YOUR JUSTICE JOURNEY:

Your imagination is your greatest asset. Within our minds, we can visualize whatever we choose and witness whatever comes to us from our internal world. That's right. We have an internal world within us filled with answers and information for us to reap.

Do the following exercise at your pace, and if you are not familiar with visualization, there is no right or wrong way. Allow it to be what it is. Everyone is unique.

The best way to approach inner visualization is to relax and breathe. Your answers will come more quickly and clearly if you stop trying or expecting what the answer may be and instead allow it to come to you. Soon, you will be amazed at the information you receive.

The great news is that whatever experience you have within your visualization is powerful enough to bring healing and inner peace for whatever happened in your past because it will create empowering meaning for any event, which trumps the negative story we created about ourselves having gone through that experience.

1. Close your eyes and imagine that you are traveling back in time to gather some Red Flags that showed themselves in an experience that later proved hurtful. Look for both the Red Flags you heeded and the ones you ignored. Don't judge or beat yourself up; this exercise is to gain clarity and compassion for who you were back then, the investment you had in your relationship, the hope you

held onto, and the fear you had that kept you holding on. Consider it a scavenger hunt and imagine you are embarking on an adventure.

2. As you take this walk back in time, visualize yourself as a powerful, wise, evolved version of yourself, someone who has all the pieces to their journey puzzle and knows with certainty their greatness and who they are meant to be in the world. This part of you is bold, empowered, determined, intentional and focused on finding resolution and closure for this experience in your past, so that you can move forward toward a joyful, peaceful, full life. Imagine what this powerful part of you looks like. What are you wearing? What is the energy you carry and the purpose you hold? Refer to this part of you as your Wise Self.

3. Imagine your Wise Self is walking back in your past, and have your Past Self, the part of you who in the past had the experience, join your Wise Self. Together, look back and find at least one or two Red Flags in this experience. Something you saw, had suspicions about, felt there was something steering you in a different direction or something you were lying to yourself about. Once you see this clearly, open your eyes and write about it on a piece of paper or in your journal. Don't

censor yourself and be radically honest. Now is the time to clear up the obstacles that are in your way of living your intended life. Once you've written down what you see, close your eyes and breathe.

4. Imagine now, your Wise Self having a conversation with your Past Self. What does your Wise Self want to say about the Red Flags of this experience? What do they tell your Past Self is the lesson of this experience and what do they want you to know about this time of your life that can support you in your life today? Don't get frustrated if you're not seeing your Wise Self clearly or getting answers. Just breathe and allow. This isn't a test, and you won't be graded. If I asked you to imagine a balloon of your favorite color, you would see it. Just breathe and imagine. Once you get answers from your Wise Self, open your eyes and write them down in your journal.

5. Now that your Wise Self has shared with you, share with them what you wished you had done differently then and what you would do differently today with what you now know. Is there something you wished you said to the person or people involved in this experience? Is there something you wished you did or didn't do? Share with your Wise Self. Keep in

mind that your Wise Self isn't here to judge you, but to support you. They are a powerful part of you, and they have your best interest at heart. They want to help you clean your inner world of any negative energy around this experience and claim your best life. Open your eyes and take some notes.

6. Close your eyes once again and imagine that your Wise Self is creating the scenario you just shared with them, and you now can visualize this experience saying and doing whatever you would have liked to do back then. This is your moment to get the justice you would have liked. Breathe. If you get emotional, don't fight it. There is no greater release than a good cry. If you get angry, let it be. Visualize whatever it is you need to have closure. If you want to imagine them getting what's owed them, go for it. Give yourself the opportunity to go back in time and do things differently in the safety of your internal world. Get your justice because, from this day forward, it will be about embracing your Wise Self within you and living differently, by setting boundaries, implementing consequences, confronting others, demanding respect and trusting in the Karma Gods. When you are complete, open your eyes and write about it.

7. Close your eyes for the last time in this exercise and send thanks to both your Past Self, who I hope you have some deep compassion and self-forgiveness for, and your Wise Self, who is here to support you now and going forward. Take any additional notes and breathe.

8. Give yourself a hug.

You can go directly to the F**k You Declaration or take a break and come back to it later. And even though the Declaration is powerful after completing The Justice Journey, it can be done without doing the Justice Journey exercise. The F**k You Declaration is powerful on its own.

Allow me to preface this next step with saying that I place the asterisks in F**k, as to not offend anyone. I must admit there is no other phrase in the English language that I can think of that has more meaning and leverage behind it than F**k You. It is loaded with emotion, it's bold and it feels good to say it and freely feel it. I am a firm believer that the people who shy away from using it think about it and feel it inside. And the intention of this book is to feel, see, hear, express.

The intention of this declaration is for the *You* in F**k You to stand in for all OBSTACLES, whatever is in your way of living your best life. It may be a person, a thing, a thought, a belief, an experience, a situation, anything that's using your energy and keeps you from living the life that you want.

For example, if I carry the belief that I am not good enough, the *You* in F**k You would be the belief. If I'm angry at my friend Sally, and I'm ruminating about her and it's holding me back from peace and joy, the *You* would be referring to Sally.

Again, this is a way to release toxic negativity so that we can get back to living well. For there is no greater payback than rising to greater heights despite what's happened to us.

THE F**K YOU DECLARATION

On this day, (fill in the blank), I, (your name), declare to myself, to all the others involved and to the world, that I will no longer allow you, (fill in the obstacle), to take away my joy, affect my energy, or impact my peace in any way.

On this day, I declare that you, (fill in the obstacle), will no longer take over my mind with negative thoughts and rumination that keep me away from my creativity and productivity.

I furthermore declare that there's no longer any value or benefit, positive or negative, in holding on to you, and I am therefore choosing to let you go, but not without holding you partly responsible for my pain and distress.

As I release you, I want to make it clear that I do not condone anything, and that even though I am willing to let go, I will not do so without letting you know how I feel about you and am sending you off with a bold farewell.

So, F**k YOU, (fill in the blank), and know this: As thankful as I am for all that you've taught me, I deserve better and you don't deserve me, my attention, my love, my greatness, my friendship, my support or my giving you another moment of my day.

F**K YOU, (fill in the blank), and may you rest assured that you have no more place in my heart, in my life, in my mind or in my journey.

I am free of you, (fill in the blank).

_____

Signature

*Walk powerfully forward and use your voice.
Follow your guidance and you will rejoice.
The Red Flags are here to show you the way.
Salute them and listen to all that they say.*

As an Emotional Wellness Coach for fourteen years, Eve supports her clients to step into their lives with both feet.

Honoring her own journey, filled with both heartache and joy, Eve knows that living one's intended life is essential to find meaning and purpose. She believes whole-heartedly that self-forgiveness and following inner guidance is the way.

BOOKS BY EVE ROSENBERG:

My Dearest Self, I forgive you: The Essential Steps to Embracing Your Journey and Loving Your Life

Your Happy Life Realized: How to Stop Putting Others First and Yourself Last NOW!

Be Selfish, Eat Well, Serve Many: Taking the Path to Your Happiest Life

I Don't Want to Take Care of My Mother: How to Forgive the Woman Who Neglected You

To learn more, visit www.howtobelieveinyou.com.

www.ingramcontent.com/pod-product-compliance
Lightning Source LLC
Chambersburg PA
CBHW060458030426
42337CB00015B/1642